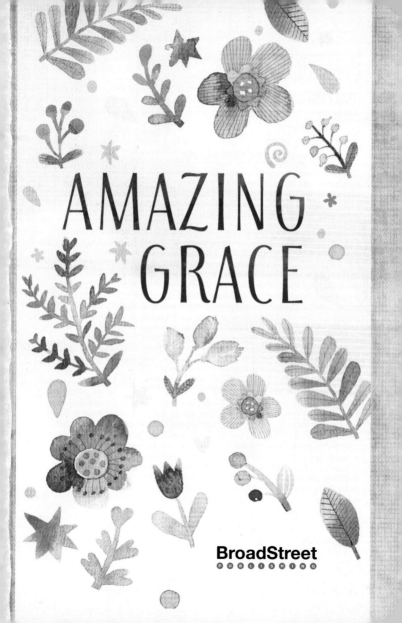

AMAZING GRACE

BroadStreet
PUBLISHING

BroadStreet Publishing Group, LLC.
Savage, Minnesota, USA
Broadstreetpublishing.com

AMAZING GRACE

978-1-4245-6024-0
978-1-4245-6025-7 (ebook)

Devotional entries composed by Brenna Stockman.

The faithful love
of the LORD never ends!
His mercies never cease.
Great is his faithfulness;
His mercies begin afresh
each morning.

LAMENTATIONS 3:22-23 NLT

INTRODUCTION

The circumstances of life may have you feeling overwhelmed, frustrated, or discouraged, but God's love isn't dependent on your situation. Because his love for you is unchanging and his promises are true, you can choose to believe in the steady outpouring of grace he has for you from the minute you wake up to the moment you lay down to sleep.

Find the hope, joy, and strength that is abundant in God as you reflect on these devotional entries, scriptures, and prayers. Claim his grace over your life and continue to believe that your Creator loves you deeply no matter what comes your way.

JANUARY

"My grace is all you need.
My power works best in weakness."

2 CORINTHIANS 12:9 NLT

SEEK HIS FACE

Look to the LORD and his strength;
seek his face always.
1 CHRONICLES 16:11 NIV

It can be difficult to ask for help at times, and we like to try to solve our problems on our own. That is not how the Lord created us to operate. We need his strength to persevere, and we need the support of others as well.

Rather than trying to muster up enough power to forge through life alone, we should seek the Lord's face and ask for help in times of trouble. The Lord is gracious and generous. He gives us strength, and he also gives us each other.

Lord, I will seek your face always! When I feel overwhelmed and incapable of carrying on, I will come before you and ask for strength. Humble me to ask others for help when I need it and give me eyes to see when someone else may need my help.

Who has the Lord put in your life that has been a source of strength and encouragement for you?

VICTORY IN CHRIST

The God of peace will soon crush Satan under your feet.
The grace of our Lord Jesus be with you.

ROMANS 16:20 NIV

As we continue to follow the ways of truth and godliness, the enemy also persists in his attempts to thwart us. Paul warned the people of false teachers and doctrine, which is one of the devil's crafty ways of undermining the work of Christ and Christians. God gives us the promise, however, that these attacks will ultimately fail and our enemy will be struck down! Everything that is a lie will fall away and only what is true will remain.

Through all of life's trials and the deception of others, we are given the promise that Jesus' grace will be with us. All the calamity and lies of the world cannot derail us from following Christ when we have been given the gifts of grace, peace, and truth.

Thank you for your grace, Lord Jesus. Thank you for standing up for me and protecting me from the enemy's attempts to destroy me. You are my victory and I find great peace in your promise of deliverance.

How do Paul's words associate with God's prophetic promise in Genesis 3:15?

LOYAL LOVE

Hold on to loyal love and don't let go, and be faithful to all that you've been taught. Let your life be shaped by integrity, with truth written upon your heart.

PROVERBS 3:3 TPT

The Lord's loyalty toward us and his love for us is unbreakable! That same love and loyalty that he pours on us he also places in us. Our sinful natures can at times take over, but when we focus on how God truly remade us and fashioned us in his love, we find that he is the one who helps us live out our true selves.

We must hold fast to this love, be faithful to God, and act in the way he has taught us to. Reading his Word and taking his lessons to heart will imprint his integrity and truth on us.

Your loyal love overwhelms me, Father, it is unfathomable. The enemy tries to disrupt it, but you have always remained faithful to your people even to the point of death on a cross. Thank you for this incredible gift.

How do you hold on to loyal love?

MINDSET OF CHRIST

In your relationships with one another, have the same mindset as Christ Jesus: Who, being in very nature God, did not consider equality with God something to be used to his own advantage and being found in appearance as a man, he humbled himself by becoming obedient to death—even death on a cross!

PHILIPPIANS 2:5-6, 8 NIV

The attitude Christ bore was one of servanthood and sacrifice. His humble obedience is meant to serve as a model for us to replicate. If the King of the universe is willing to overlook his grandiose rights for the sake of love, and subject himself to all the mistreatment of the world, then we can also partake in serving others in the relationships God has given us.

Whatever our current calling, we know we are walking with a God who understands.

Lord, help me to embrace the relationships you have given me with the same attitude you have. Whether I am loving my spouse, parents, children, friends, neighbors, bosses, or strangers, I want to love them the way you loved me.

As you find yourself in situations that require Christlike servanthood, do you embrace them with a humble and obedient mindset as well?

DELIGHT IN THE LAW

Blessed is the man who walks not in the counsel of the wicked,
nor stands in the way of sinners, nor sits in the seat of scoffers;
but his delight is in the law of the Lord,
and on his law he meditates day and night.

PSALM 1:1-2 ESV

We walk in truth and in the light, so our actions are transparent and we invite accountability. We study the Word of God and find our delight in it, for it reveals truth to us.

There is a big difference in sitting with the sinner and sitting in "the way" of the sinner. Jesus sat with sinners; in fact, he sought them out. We are called to love the lost and even to welcome them into our lives. We are not supposed to act the way they do or delight in their wrongdoing. We identify ourselves with Christ and mimic his ways which were always good and pure.

Oh God, your way is the only way. I will choose to walk the way you walked and ponder your words day and night. Your Scriptures are my guide and the blueprint for my life.

What delights you about the law of the Lord?

COMFORT

"Blessed are the poor in spirit, for theirs is the kingdom of heaven. Blessed are those who mourn, for they will be comforted."

MATTHEW 5:3-4 NIV

Poverty is not simply an economic hardship, it can be a spiritual one too. The phrase "blessed are the poor" has become well-known, but when Jesus first spoke it, it was outrageous! The term "blessing" in those days was synonymous with wealth; it was not simply a spiritual virtue.

Jesus came to turn the tables and change the world's systems. Although the planet still suffers under the weight of sin, another law has been set in motion which we, as Christians, are devoted to above any other law. The law of Christ is love. Love God and love others. The poor in spirit will not be cast out or ostracized; in fact, the kingdom of heaven is theirs! Those who mourn will find comfort in Christ.

You are my comfort when I mourn. My tears and my suffering are not forever, but you and your kingdom are. You are my blessing and my richness, dearest Lord.

What comforts you when you mourn?

PERFECT PEACE

You will keep him in perfect peace,
whose mind is stayed on You,
because he trusts in You.

ISAIAH 26:3 NKJV

Not only does the Lord reward those who trust in him with peace, but that is also the obvious outcome of having a God-centered mind. This world is full of trouble and mishap. If we focus on our problems, we are bound to become anxious. Even if we focus on ourselves, our inadequacies can become our impending apprehension.

By focusing on God and truly trusting in his ability to overcome every problem, our hearts and minds can be at peace because we know we are secure in his love and his capable hands. There is no problem too big for the Lord to lead us through it.

Father, fill me with your peace. My focus is on you and I eagerly soak up your words. You have covered me with your love and given me your joy. I know you will also preserve me with your perfect peace if I put my trust in you.

How do you maintain focus on God when life is piling on problems?

LACKING WISDOM

If any of you lacks wisdom, you should ask God, who gives generously to all without finding fault, and it will be given to you.

JAMES 1:5 NIV

It is easy to say we want wisdom and to ask God for it, but when those difficult decisions come and we feel trapped between a rock and a hard place, what we truly rely on becomes evident. Do we trust ourselves first? Would we rather follow the systems of this world? Or is our first response to turn to God's Word and prayer?

The Lord promises to supply what we're lacking and give us the answers we need. He does not treat us with disdain for our lack of wisdom but invites us to partake in his.

Please help me to trust you in any and all of life's circumstances, dear Father. May I turn to you for wisdom rather than myself or the world. You are always faithful to answer and deliver on your promises, and your generosity is limitless.

Can you think of a time when the wisdom of God was in direct conflict with the teachings of this world? How did you proceed? What was the outcome?

TRUE LIFE

This is how God showed his love to us: He sent his one and only Son into the world so that we could have life through him.

1 JOHN 4:9 NCV

The Bible is so clear that Jesus is God's Son and that true life is found only through him. It says that God sent him, implying that he came here from elsewhere. Jesus was not simply born here like the rest of us; he existed before time with God and as God. They are one together and divine in nature.

Being sent also indicates that Jesus had been given a mission. He was not on a casual visit to earth, but on an assignment to demonstrate God's love for us, his complete dominance over death and all evil realms, and to free us from every form of bondage by taking it on himself.

Oh Jesus, I am in awe of your love and compassion! You are my God and King, wholly deserving of my love and devotion. Thank you for your gifts, your sacrifice, and the life you have so lovingly given to me.

How does this verse remind you that love is more than a feeling; it demonstrates actions and change?

SUREFOOTED

God arms me with strength,
and he makes my way perfect.
He makes me as surefooted as a deer,
enabling me to stand on mountain heights.
He trains my hands for battle;
he strengthens my arm to draw a bronze bow.
PSALM 18:32-34 NLT

When we are walking God's way, we can be as surefooted as a deer because we will not question the integrity of our steps. Even on a high mountain, we do not need to fear because we know that the Lord is guiding us.

God has trained our hands and our feet to operate according to his will, and so whatever comes our way we know that we have the strength to face it.

Lord, you are the skip in my step! Not only am I confident because you are my diligent guide, but I experience so much joy following you. You make me surefooted and strong, capable of facing anything that tries to distract me from pursuing you.

Does walking in God's perfect way mean you will not face trouble? Why does God give you strength and train your hands for battle?

CRY AND LAUGH

There is a time to cry and a time to laugh.
There is a time to be sad and a time to dance.
ECCLESIASTES 3:4 NCV

Sometimes in life we experience heartache. To deny how we feel and attempt to go about our lives as if nothing has happened can be harmful. The Lord wants to lead us through the hard times not around them. He is prepared to be our Comforter, but we must first admit that we need the comfort.

There is also a time to surrender our sadness to the Lord and get back up again. There are some things we cannot simply stop feeling, but we also cannot let them keep us down. Embracing our laughing and our dancing again is not denying the sad times; it is choosing to press forward in the comfort and love of God.

I recognize that there are times to cry and times to laugh, and both are important. You yourself, dear God, have cried and laughed. Please give me courage to embark on both paths when it is time and lead me through them by your love.

Do you struggle with transitioning between sadness and feeling happy again? Have you asked God to guide you?

STRENGTH

Be strong in the Lord and in his mighty power.
EPHESIANS 6:10 NLT

Paul did not undercut the importance of the spiritual battles we engage with. He wrote often about how we are in a war against evil and cautioned us to be alert to it. Just prior to describing a detailed metaphor of suiting up in spiritual armor with each of its specific components, he gave the most necessary piece of battleplan advice: "Be strong in the Lord."

God is ready and willing to give us everything we need for any situation. Often, however, he will wait for us to ask so we are reminded that he is our source of strength and that we should always be turned toward him.

I am inadequate and overwhelmed without you, God. Your strength and power are what win the battles and even what carries me through each day. When I am attacked or confronted with evil, please equip me with your strength and your spiritual armor so I remember that, despite my inadequacy, I am not helpless because you are with me.

What other battleplans does the book of Ephesians offer?

PATIENCE

Whoever is patient has great understanding,
but one who is quick-tempered displays folly.
PROVERBS 14:29 NIV

One of the best ways to learn is to listen. When we are hasty and quick to anger, we fail to glean any further understanding about the situation. Even if we are correct in our anger, there may be pieces of the controversy that we have not yet realized. Perhaps there are things we cannot see.

Whatever the case, we have an obligation to conduct ourselves as Christ would, and his patience in the face of injustice and controversy is resolute. To act in any other way is to demonstrate foolishness before God and others. Practicing patience will increase our understanding.

Lord, I ask for patience and greater understanding. When I feel attacked or offended, please help me to hold back my anger and pray. Reveal to me your better way and guide my mouth to speak truth into every situation.

When did Jesus display patience in the Bible?

GENTLE SPIRIT

Let it be the hidden person of the heart,
with the imperishable quality of a gentle and quiet spirit,
which is precious in the sight of God.

1 PETER 3:4 NASB

Writing specifically to Christian wives, Peter cautioned that women find their true worth and beauty in their unseen character rather than outward appearance. As women, we are daily inundated with messages about our appearance and given insurmountable standards. Rather than striving to achieve some form of impossible physique, our focus should be on cultivating a humble and quiet heart.

Peter is not commanding women to stay quiet but to possess a quiet spirit. To obtain this necessitates a level of peace and contentment. It means overcoming anxiety and strife, faithfully leaning on God in every aspect of life, and choosing to be gentle like Christ. It's often easier to harden our hearts. In a world that praises impenetrable toughness, we need to choose to follow the example of Christ who was literally pierced for the sake of love.

Lord, it is so much easier to allow my heart to grow hard and hide behind a cover of not caring. Instead, I pray that you keep me gentle and loving; keep my heart open to weep and laugh and learn. I desire to be precious in your sight.

If not silence, what are the outward signs of a gentle and quiet spirit?

TEMPERED ANGER

Be angry, and do not sin;
ponder in your own hearts on your beds,
and be silent.
PSALM 4:4 ESV

Anger is not in itself a sin but acting malicious and impulsively is. Often the Lord is angered, but his reactions are always calculated and loving. He can see the big picture, and we cannot. Rather than act on our anger, the Bible encourages us to ponder it and opt to stay silent.

Once submitted to the Lord, we will know how to proceed, but rarely is our reaction loving when anger is newly stirring in our hearts. Taking time to contemplate the matter and pray will help us gain perspective and keep from sinning.

Help me in my anger, Lord. Keep my mouth and heart from sinning. I will bring every matter before you and ask for your wisdom, then I will follow your example in how I proceed. Fill me with love for others and may peace be the outcome I am striving for.

In the moment something angers you, how can you stay tempered and keep from sinning?

OVERCOME THE WORLD

"I have told you these things, so that in me you may have peace.
In this world you will have trouble. But take heart!
I have overcome the world."

JOHN 16:33 NIV

There is no evil in this world that Christ has not already overcome. He has accounted for everything that may happen to us and guarantees that we can overcome it through his power. We can take heart and have confidence knowing that we also have secured victory because of the Lord Jesus' resurrection.

God has related his plan to us so we may have peace knowing that our future with him is guaranteed. Regardless of what terrible situations we face in this life, they will pass away. Christ's kingdom is lasting and his victory is forever.

You are the Prince of Peace and you have truly overcome the world! I also experience your peace because of the victory I am promised through you. Calm my heart when it wanders or forgets your truth, Lord Jesus, and help me to remember my position in your eternal kingdom.

What trials shake your peace and cause you to doubt?
How has Christ demonstrated that he has also overcome
these trials?

FOUNTAIN OF SALVATION

With joy you will drink deeply from the fountain of salvation!
ISAIAH 12:3 NLT

The Lord refreshes the hearts of those who choose to seek him. Not only does salvation save our souls, but it constantly rejuvenates us. God is not simply interested in numbers of followers but of cultivating a loving relationship with each of us.

Our caring Father walks with us daily, listens to our prayers, intervenes on our behalf, and orchestrates everything for our good. When we are weary, we can turn to him, our Creator and Comforter, and drink from the fountain of his salvation. He did not fashion us and then leave us on our own; he is our Savior as well as our sustainer.

Father, I come before you thirsty, and you never fail to quench my thirst. Over and over I return to your fountain because your grace never runs dry. Your love pours over and I am flooded with your joy.

Do you view your salvation as a one-time gift, or as the beginning of a loving and active relationship?

ABILITY

We are not saying that we can do this work ourselves.
It is God who makes us able to do all that we do.

2 CORINTHIANS 3:5 NCV

When the Lord gives us a mission, he does not intend for us to obediently march forward in it alone, like impersonal soldiers. His invitation is to go forth with him, working together, and growing more and more in love with each other. There is no work the Lord has called us to that he will not also equip us for.

God trains us and prepares us when we cultivate an active relationship with him. We are incapable of living a holy life without him, so it is important that we stay aware of our need for him and turn to him in the good times and the bad.

My ability comes from you, Lord God. You train me, teach me, and raise me up. Like a loving Father, you are always nearby, imparting wisdom and showing me the way. Thank you for the work you have given me to do and the purpose you have brought to my life.

What abilities has the Lord given you?

BANISHING BITTERNESS

Look after each other so that none of you fails to receive the grace of God. Watch out that no poisonous root of bitterness grows up to trouble you, corrupting many.

HEBREWS 12:15 NLT

We carry more of a mantle than to simply look out for our own wellbeing, but also for the welfare of others. Peace and holiness are often achieved in our interactions with others, rather than when we are simply undisturbed.

We cannot tolerate bitterness remaining in our bodies and wreaking havoc in our lives. Unforgiveness is in direct dissention of God, so how can we presume to have his protection and blessing if we live contrary to his commands?

Lift my face, Lord, so I recognize the plights others around me are facing, rather than becoming too engrossed in my own. As part of a body of believers, direct me to care for others and to truly be your hands and feet on the earth.

Who is this verse's warning about failing to receive God's grace speaking to?

DEFENDER

The LORD defends those who suffer;
he defends them in times of trouble.
Those who know the LORD trust him,
because he will not leave those who come to him.

PSALM 9:9-10 NCV

In this cruel world, those who suffer have somewhere to turn. When injustice seems to be all around us, God defends the oppressed. This world does not offer lasting hope, but the Lord extends his hand to whoever needs it, pulling them out of the mud and reestablishing them on his unshakable truth.

If we run to God, he guarantees us a place of refuge and rest, and he will never abandon his children.

Father, my home is with you. It is you who sets the captives free, heals the broken, and defends the weak. I can bring all my suffering and mistreatment to you because you care. My suffering may not end yet, but I know that you are standing with me, giving me the strength to endure, and creating something beautiful out of my brokenness.

What do you need to be defended against? Do you trust the Lord to protect you?

BE PATIENT

Always be humble and gentle. Be patient with each other,
making allowance for each other's faults because of your love.

EPHESIANS 4:2 NLT

Although we serve one God and share one faith, we are each created uniquely. Rather than reject and reprove the faults of others, we should use our strengths to help others in their weaknesses. In turn, other believers may help us when we are struggling.

The trademarks of a true Christian are clearly communicated here. We are to be humble, gentle, patient, and loving. Over and over Christ demonstrated these characteristics, even when it was not fair, convenient, or reciprocated. As his followers, we are called to live the same way. This is how the world will recognize who Christ really is.

Lord Jesus, you chose to live humbly, yet your life impacted the entire world and still does to this day. With your testimony as my example, please help me to walk as you walked. I will choose the humble path as well.

What is the difference between making allowances for each other's faults and endorsing sin?

DEVOTION

*They were continually devoting themselves to the apostles'
teaching and to fellowship, to the breaking of bread and to prayer.*
ACTS 2:42 NASB

The devil has an agenda and so does the Lord. The one is bent on destruction while the other is devoted to loving us. The choice to do nothing is to simply accept the systems of this world with all its self-gratification and spiritual numbness. The early believers understood that there was a war being waged for their souls, so they diligently took to heart the apostles' teaching and fellowship with other believers.

We were designed for community because we are stronger together. By fellowshipping, sharing communion, and praying together, we invite others to have an active role in our lives. We enjoy our time together, but we also confess our sins and our weaknesses. We bear each other's burdens and stay devoted through the good times and bad.

Thank you for establishing a family of believers who I can turn to in times of trouble. Sometimes other people can be very difficult, so please help me humble my heart to walk in service to you.

Who have you opened your spiritual life to? Who knows your struggles and your successes?

DISCIPLINE FOR LIFE

He who heeds discipline shows the way to life,
but whoever ignores correction leads others astray.
PROVERBS 10:17 NIV

Rarely do our decisions affect us alone. Sin and love both have a way of multiplying. The Lord disciplines those he loves because he cares about our betterment. If we are humble enough to receive his loving discipline and grow from it, we can use our spiritual maturity and our learned lessons as a gift to others. Having a faith that we can share is an incredible thing!

If we live unwilling to learn or yield, it can be to our detriment and the detriment of others. This is especially true with leaders in the church, teachers, and parents.

Convict me of your holiness, dear God, and keep my heart from growing hard. I want to hear your voice and respond. Thank you for not allowing me to wander alone but correcting me and keeping me safely on your straight and narrow path.

Has the Lord corrected or disciplined you lately? How did you respond? Did it make you feel loved?

LOVE

Love is patient and kind. Love is not jealous,
it does not brag, and it is not proud.
1 CORINTHIANS 13:4 NCV

The love Paul is describing in this eloquent, poetic, well-known passage is agape love. It is different than brotherly love (phileo) or romantic love (eros). Agape love is godly love. Paul took great care in accurately delving into the attributes of agape love, and describing it in detail to the self-centered Corinthians.

Agape love is not a mere feeling but an action-oriented lifestyle that we choose when we make the decision to follow God. Love means exercising patience and kindness and resisting jealousy and pride.

Thank you for your patient and kind agape love toward me, dear Father! Thank you for filling me with that same love and sending me out as your beloved child to a lost and loveless world. Rather than bragging about what I have or being jealous of what I don't, help me to recognize the incredible gift that love is. I want to joyfully share it with everyone.

How can you demonstrate agape love to those closest to you today? Name some specific ways.

HEAR MY VOICE

Lord, every morning you hear my voice.
Every morning, I tell you what I need,
and I wait for your answer.

PSALM 5:3 NCV

There is not a single day when the Lord is not active in your life and attentive to your voice. He is constantly guiding and guarding, fulfilling your needs, and answering your questions. At times, it may seem like he is silent or that your needs are great, but the Lord does not view matters the same way we do.

God is answering the deeper questions and fulfilling our greater needs. Every morning, we can be assured that he hears our every prayer and will go through the day with us.

Lord, thank you for hearing my voice and responding. Sometimes you respond in a way I do not like or did not expect, but that is because I see things temporarily from a fixed point in time. You have a much greater plan and perspective. Please help me to be patient and trust you fully.

In the mornings when you are thinking about the day ahead, what do you ask God for?

LISTEN AND OBEY

"Blessed rather are those who hear the word of God and obey it."
LUKE 11:28 NIV

How can we call Jesus our king if we do not obey what he says? What good is it to know the Scriptures if we do not follow their teachings? Out of our great love for Jesus and our devotion to him, we must study the Word of God. We should take it to heart and live our lives based on its message.

If anyone has the answers and knows the truth, yet they choose to live otherwise, how can their lives be blessed? They have regarded their own wisdom as superior to God's. Those who listen to the Word of God and also obey it will experience God's blessings because they are choosing the wiser path.

Lord, incline my ears to your truth, and give me understanding as I study your Word. As I go forward through life, I pray that you help me be obedient to the instructions I have received. May I walk in love toward you and others.

What is an example of being obedient to God's Word?

REWARDS

*"I the LORD search the heart and examine the mind,
to reward each person according to their conduct,
according to what their deeds deserve."*

JEREMIAH 17:10 NIV

We cannot hide our true intentions or heart motives from God, for he made us and knows us each intimately. He understands us completely and loves us immeasurably! He wants to give good gifts to his children, to reward us for our obedience, and to praise our good deeds.

Like a proud Father, God searches our hearts and minds, and he delights in our faith. Even when we feel like our deeds may be small or insignificant, our heavenly Father finds pleasure in them.

It is bewildering to me, Father, that you find pleasure in me. I am so unworthy of your love, yet you lavishly adore me and reward even my most feeble attempts. You encourage me and pick me up when I fall. Even when my faith seems weak, you take it and make something beautiful out of it. Please, search my heart and my mind, and continue to find pleasure in me.

How have you sought to please the Lord lately?

COMFORT AND STRENGTH

May our Lord Jesus Christ himself and God our Father, who loved us and by his grace gave us eternal comfort and a wonderful hope, comfort you and strengthen you in every good thing you do and say.

2 THESSALONIANS 2:16-17 NLT

After being confused about when the Lord Jesus would return, and after facing extreme persecution, the Thessalonians needed the Lord's refreshing hope, comfort, and strength. By God's grace, they were able to face every obstacle with confidence and strength. In every action and every word, they were able to choose to do good. Nothing was too much for them because God had demonstrated his love to them.

We also can face all things and cling to what is good. Whenever we feel hopeless, tired, weak, or confused, we can find all the refreshment we need in Christ Jesus. He is our hope and our strength, our eternal comfort, and perfect lover.

Dearest Lord Jesus, thank you for your comfort and strength. There is nothing that can steal me away from you or overpower me because you are with me and your grace is sufficient. I cling to you today and every day.

How can you find comfort in uncomfortable times?

COMMANDMENTS

These commandments that I give you today are to be on your hearts. Impress them on your children. Talk about them when you sit at home and when you walk along the road, when you lie down and when you get up.

DEUTERONOMY 6:6-7 NIV

It is one thing to understand the commandments of God, and quite another to craft a life upon them. They are to be the compass of our lives, not a mere plaque on the wall. Others should be well aware of the commandments because of the impression we leave on them. The way we live is a testimony to what we believe, and others see us very clearly.

These commandments should be in our conversations at home and in how we do business out of the home. The way we start our days and the way we end our days should be as obedient children of a God who cares enough to give us his commandments.

Thank you for your commandments, God. You have given me guidelines to keep me on the road that leads to life and to show me how to have the most potential for my life. I love your Word and I will live by it daily.

How do God's commandments define you?

TEACH AND GUIDE

Show me your ways, Lord, teach me your paths.
Guide me in your truth and teach me,
for you are God my Savior and my hope is in you all day long.
Remember, Lord, your great mercy and love,
for they are from of old.

PSALM 25:4-6 NIV

The way of the Lord leads to life and love. Any other path divulges self-seeking and lust. Our natural inclination is to follow the road of selfish gain, but the Lord interposes and guides us back to our true purpose. He is willing to show us the way and to give us all truth, but we must be willing to follow him as our God and Savior.

The Lord is not a trivial extra or a tradition. If he is not King of our lives, then we are certain to become lost. He is full of love and mercy for whoever puts their faith and hope in him alone.

Thank you for leading me in love and establishing me in your mercy. I praise you because you did not allow me to continue on the path that leads to destruction. You showed me a better way.

How does God teach and guide you?

EVERYTHING

His divine power has given us everything we need for a godly life through our knowledge of him who called us by his own glory and goodness.

2 PETER 1:3 NIV

Although we may be fully equipped, we still have to choose to use the gifts God has given us. He has given us everything we need, and he has also called us. We need to respond to that call.

Peter stresses the point that it is by God's divine power that we have received the ability to lead a godly life. We were not born with this capacity since it was given to us, and we did not earn godly aptitude since it was a gift by his glory and goodness alone. We receive all that we require by knowing him.

Draw me closer, God, and teach me more about you every day. Even at this very moment, I am aware that you have given me everything I need for a godly life, so I will rise up and live out your glorious gift.

Why did Peter think it was so important that his readers understand they are already equipped for every good work and in possession of everything they need?

FEBRUARY

God saved you by his grace
when you believed.
And you can't take credit for this;
it is a gift from God.

EPHESIANS 2:8 NLT

GIVEN LIFE

You gave me life and showed me kindness,
and in your care you watched over my life.
JOB 10:12 NCV

Our heavenly Father does not simply create life and then abandon it. Every day he is gently guiding us and caring for our needs. He is a kind God who is constantly watching over us. He created each of us out of love and for a purpose. His heart aches over those who have rejected him and rejoices for those who have accepted his love!

The image of an impartial, far off deity is often falsely prescribed to him, but that does not depict his character at all. In the beginning, the Lord walked with humans in a perfect paradise, and it is his desire to do so again.

Lord God, your kindness reaches further than my comprehension. Your love for me is immeasurable and complete. There is nothing good lacking in your character. I thank you for creating me, but also for caring for me every day.

What were Job's circumstances while he proclaimed these words?

FAITH

Faith comes from hearing, and hearing by the word of Christ.
ROMANS 10:17 NASB

Although Israel had been given countless prophesies, teaching, and signs, they refused to recognize Jesus as their Messiah. They continued to strive to achieve righteousness by upholding the law and failed to realize that Jesus Christ was the completion of the law: all of God's laws were in place to point to Christ.

So fixated were the people on the letter of the law that they overlooked its message of love. At the core of their unbelief, there existed an unwillingness to accept the truth. It is imperative that we humble ourselves to accept Christ's free and undeserved gift of salvation by the power of his Word.

I hear your words, and I accept your truth. My Messiah, thank you for opening my ears and my heart. I put my faith fully in you again today and every day.

Do you sometimes get caught up attempting to achieve righteousness by your own merit? How did God respond to Israel when they acted this way, according to Romans 10:21? How does he respond to you?

GENTLE ANSWER

A gentle answer will calm a person's anger,
but an unkind answer will cause more anger.

PROVERBS 15:1 NCV

Although the facts may stand, delivery is foundational. When someone engages us angrily, our instinct is an angry rebuttal. Our walls come up because we do not feel safe, and our irritation begins to surface. To return anger for anger, however, only heightens emotions and does not solve the problems.

In these moments, we can remember what the Lord Jesus did when confronted with angry individuals or even angry mobs. He remained calm, spoke truth, and nobody could ever find fault in him. His wise and gentle answers left people baffled and touched their hearts. Regardless of whether the situation is fair or not, we need to follow Jesus' example if we want to see lives changed.

Please fill my heart with gentleness, God, and help me recognize what a powerful tool it is. More than I want to retaliate, I want to see hearts changed. I want people to recognize you in me.

What are some things you can do to remain calm when someone approaches you angrily?

REJOICE

Rejoice in the Lord always. I will say it again: Rejoice!
PHILIPPIANS 4:4 NIV

True joy is so much more than mere happiness. As Christians, we rejoice because of the hope we have in Jesus. There will come a day when all our suffering and sorrows will be wiped away and we will finally be at home with our Lord. Understanding this powerful truth should fill us with a continual joy that is more real than our circumstances.

We should not overlook that when Paul penned these words, he was in jail for being wrongly accused. Just prior to his imprisonment, he had been shipwrecked, bitten by a snack, and placed under house arrest. Yet because of how aware he was of his eternal inheritance, nothing was able to steal his joy.

Father, amid my hardships and heartbreaks, I will cling to your hope and choose joy. Even in my sadness, remind me of what awaits me.

Do you think it is more difficult to choose to rejoice in horrible circumstances, or to remember to rejoice throughout the mundane activities of daily life? Why is joy always important?

LOOKING FORWARD

We do not look at what we can see right now, the troubles all around us, but we look forward to the joys in heaven which we have not yet seen. The troubles will soon be over, but the joys to come will last forever.

2 CORINTHIANS 4:18 TLB

In this world, there is much trouble. Relationships are tricky, our bodies decay, and finances chase us unrelentingly. Evil extends to all corners of the earth. All these things will fade away, however, and only what you have established will remain.

All the troubles that we face daily may plague us now, but they cannot steal our joy. We gaze forward to your coming and are reminded of the temporality of our difficulties.

Forward, dear Father, is the only path for me. There are days when the fight seems so intense, the path so lonely, and my sorrow so consuming, but you continue to lead me forward. Help me to be brave and to set my eyes on you. The joys awaiting me do not compare to the distress I experience now.

How does a proper perspective change the way you walk?

SERVE

*"The Son of Man did not come to be served, but to serve,
and to give His life a ransom for many."*
MATTHEW 20:28 NASB

Jesus had every right to demand the allegiance and servitude of the world, but he chose the difficult road of love. Instead of requiring payment for our disobedience, he paid the price. By coming to earth and serving mankind, he demonstrated that his love for us was more important to him than his rights. He left his throne to suffer on our behalf.

In the same manner, we are constantly confronted with opportunities to choose ourselves or to choose others. If our greatest desires are for our own rights, comfort, and safety, then we are not walking like Jesus did.

Grow my capacity to love, Lord Jesus. I want to serve others like you did. If you, the eternal King, could choose the road of servanthood, then I can certainly humble myself and attend to the needs of others as well.

Why did Jesus choose to come to earth as a humble servant rather than as a ruling king?

HUMBLE HONOR

Pride will ruin people,
but those who are humble will be honored.

PROVERBS 29:23 NCV

Pride is the result of self-focus and a lack of love for others. The Bible reminds us many times to put others first, to be a servant of all, to lay down our rights for the sake of our sisters and brothers, and to follow in the footsteps of Christ. It is God who exalts people and honors them in his perfect timing.

If people, worthy or unworthy, are receiving praise, do not succumb to jealousy. Rather, praise God! We do not know what is in their hearts or what is in the mind of God. He works everything together for the good of those who love him, and it is his pleasure to bring honor to the humble.

I exalt you, Lord, and I praise your holy name. You alone are worthy and yet you choose to consider me. Thank you for remembering the poor and the weak, for honoring the humble, and for exalting the faithful in your own way and your own time.

How does pride ruin people?

HARVEST

No discipline seems pleasant at the time, but painful. Later on,
however, it produces a harvest of righteousness and peace for
those who have been trained by it.

HEBREWS 12:11 NIV

When we are in the middle of a difficult or painful time,
it is hard to be aware of anything other than our discomfort.
We fixate on how to get out of the situation because it is
unpleasant. In retrospect, however, we can recognize how
terrible times actually build our character and can lead us
toward a closer, more intimate relationship with God.

Instead of despising life's lessons, when we decide to learn
from them and submit ourselves to God's guidance, it can
produce an amazing amount of righteousness and peace. God
can bring forth such an abundance from the smallest offerings
of faith. To be a good disciple, we have to also be ready to
accept discipline, which is administered because of God's
great love for us.

Lord, give me a teachable spirit and a proper perspective.
Rather than rejecting opportunities for growth, I will turn
to you for comfort and hope. You are always loving and
always with me.

What are some different reasons for suffering, according to
Hebrews 12?

LOVE IN DEED

Whoever has the world's goods, and sees his brother in need and closes his heart against him, how does the love of God abide in him? Little children, let us not love with word or with tongue, but in deed and truth.

1 JOHN 3:17-18 NASB

Over and over, the writers of the Bible emphasize that love is not simply a feeling, but an action-based choice. We cannot say we love somebody and then act unlovingly or indifferent toward them. True love is evident by our deeds. To walk as Christ walked requires sacrifice.

In this verse, Peter is not telling believers to give away everything they own; he is addressing Christians who have wealth (the world's goods). When we look around and recognize someone else who is in need, and we have the ability to fill that need, we cannot allow our hearts to grow hard. If the love of God is in us, we will act as Christ demonstrated with his own love and life.

How can your love abide in me if I am not abiding in you, God? That is why I am here today, spending time with you, searching for your truth. Please fill me with your love. Then, please open my eyes to see how I can love others around me and how I can help meet their needs.

Who do you know personally that needs something? How will you help them in deed?

CONSIDERING GOD

*When I consider Your heavens, the work of Your fingers,
the moon and the stars, which you have ordained,
what is man that You are mindful of him,
and the son of man that You visit him?*

PSALM 8:3-4 NKJV

Why is it so easy for us to find such thrill and exhilaration exploring the wonders of nature, and yet so often we completely disregard the Creator who imagined all this in the first place? God is not drab or boring, he is creative and powerful. The stars were his idea. Humans will even worship the heavenly matters, such as the sun and the moon, but they are cutting themselves short.

The Lord God is far more brilliant, majestic, and exciting than any of the works of his hands. And he wants to be with us.

Creator God, I am in awe of your heavens. All your works amaze me and declare how glorious you are. Thank you for a creation that I can journey through, be enamored with, and always discover new and unsolved mysteries. You are far more incredible than all of creation. The more I come to know you, the more enamored with you I become, and the more in love with you I fall.

When was the last time you put down your phone and went outside to stare at the sky?

BANNER OF LOVE

He brought me to the banqueting house,
and his banner over me was love.
SONG OF SOLOMON 2:4 ESV

In the days of King Solomon, it was customary for the banners flown over armies to have the name of the king or the general written on them. Not only is Solomon declaring his allegiance to Christ, but he was addressing him by the name "Love."

God is not just loving; he is love itself. Although it may not always seem like it in the moment, all the plans he has for you are loving. He is a good general, a caring king, and it is of great honor to be in his army and under his banner.

I will follow you all my days, Lord of Love. I trust your leadership and your judgement, for your wisdom is far superior to any other. It is a privilege to be counted among your chosen people.

How do you feel God leading you to his banqueting hall?

SAVED BY GRACE

God is so rich in mercy, and he loved us so much,
that even though we were dead because of our sins,
he gave us life when he raised Christ from the dead.
(It is only by God's grace that you have been saved!)
EPHESIANS 2:4-5 NLT

It is important to distinguish that the difference between Christians and people who are unsaved only exists because of what God has done. When we were spiritually dead because of our sin, it was God who gave up his life and covered us with his grace and mercy. Salvation is not by our merit; we choose to accept it.

May this awareness go with you as you engage with others who hold onto their sinful ways. Your freedom was not achieved by your strength; you needed a Savior. Extend grace rather than judgment. Show love when others act unlovingly. Never forget the destitute places you came from.

You truly are rich in mercy, Lord, and generous with your grace. It is impossible to fathom the depths of your love toward me, or fully grasp the meaningfulness of your death by crucifixion. All I can say is thank you. In gratitude, I will treat other undeserving people the same way you treated me.

How can you treat others with grace today?

HUMBLE WISDOM

*When pride comes, then comes disgrace,
but with humility comes wisdom.*

PROVERBS 11:2 NIV

All too often we are eager to display our knowledge, and we are slow to listen. We open our mouths and discredit ourselves by caring more about our egos than the other people we are with. It takes wisdom to learn how to listen humbly, but in doing so we increase in wisdom and we show respect.

Others will remember how we make them feel, and it is important that they feel accepted, respected, and heard. If self-image is our aim, we will be met eventually with disgrace. If, however, our endeavors are to walk in humility and serve others, we will be the recipients of God's wisdom.

Please help me overcome my pride, dear Jesus. It is detrimental to my faith and distracts from my true calling of praising you in everything. Teach me your humble ways. I pray that you give me wisdom to know when to share and when to listen. Help me love others and cease any conceited attempts to put myself above them.

Why do pride and wisdom contradict?

GREAT MERCY

Blessed be the God and Father of our Lord Jesus Christ!
By his great mercy he has given us a new birth into a living hope
through the resurrection of Jesus Christ from the dead.

1 PETER 1:3 NRSV

Further on in this book, Peter describes the distinctions between the Father, Son, and Holy Spirit in greater detail. However, in the very beginning of this letter, he pronounces clearly their position as God and Lord: the very reason we have life and hope.

With blessing, he declares that God is the Father of Jesus, Jesus Christ is our Lord, and it was by God's mercy as well as Christ's resurrection that we have new life and a living hope. Peter left no room to question in his writing that he understood that the Father and the Son are One and they are God.

Lord Jesus, I recognize that you are and always have been the true God. You came to earth in human form, yet preceded with the Father in perfect unity. Thank you for your gift of life and for the mercy you showed me on the cross.

What are some of the descriptions that God gives in his Word to help finite minds grasp the truth of the Trinity?

FEARLESS

The LORD is my light and the one who saves me.
So why should I fear anyone?
The LORD protects my life.
So why should I be afraid?

PSALM 27:1 NCV

Darkness can be frightening because we cannot see as well and we do not know what awaits. We tend to fear what we do not know or what we cannot see. This is why those who truly know God and have a relationship with him do not need to fear the future.

Although we cannot see it, we know that God is always good and fully capable. He is a direct light upon our paths; shining with love and guidance. He illuminates the steps we need to take and we need not fear because he is our protector.

Lord, in you my hope and future is secure. Even if at times I cannot see one step ahead, I feel safe and protected because I am following you. You make me fearless by your perfect love.

In what ways does the Lord light your path? Do you worry about the future?

WORD BECAME FLESH

The Word became flesh, and dwelt among us, and we saw His glory,
glory as of the only begotten from the Father, full of grace and truth.
JOHN 1:14 NASB

Many misconceptions about Jesus were circling in John's day, so he spent the first portion of his letter correcting false doctrines. Some people said that Jesus was an illusion or a spirit disguised as a person. Others said that he was not actually God but only a mortal man or a prophet at best.

John wrote clearly that Jesus Christ came in actual flesh, which is significant because then we know that he understands our human suffering and can relate to us. Knowing this proves that there is a way for us, to journey through this world in holiness because Jesus showed us the way. John also highlighted that Jesus was begotten from the Father and embodied the glory of God. He came from God and is God in every sense of the word.

As I study your Word, Father, I become more and more aware of the truth of who you are and how great your love is. Please help me find time to truly study you so I can marvel at your glory more.

Why does John use the term the "Word" to introduce Christ?

CORNERSTONE

*Look! I am placing a foundation stone in Jerusalem, a firm and
tested stone. It is a precious cornerstone that is safe to build on.
Whoever believes need never be shaken.*

ISAIAH 28:16 NLT

Christ is the cornerstone that the whole church is built on. It
was so important in early days to find the best—the "chief"—
cornerstone because it would bear the weight of the whole
building and would either make the building straight or crooked.

Jesus Christ came and established the church. He bore the
weight of the sins of all mankind, and he is setting everything
straight again. As long as we are relying on his grace and
resting in his peace, we can have confidence that we are secure.

**Jesus, you came into my broken world and started picking
up the pieces. You healed the sick, embraced the outcasts,
bridged the gap between me and God, and fulfilled the
law. My personal journeys, my ministries, and all the work
of my hands I build on your framework. Thank you for using
broken people to conduct your mission.**

Why is it significant that Jesus is the foundation stone?

NOT DESTROYED

We have this treasure in jars of clay to show that this all-surpassing power is from God and not from us. We are hard pressed on every side, but not crushed; perplexed, but not in despair; persecuted, but not abandoned; struck down, but not destroyed.

2 CORINTHIANS 4:7-9 NIV

We are God's treasure in jars of clay. The Holy Spirit lives in us and enables us to have the power to accomplish all the Lord has called us to. This strength did not originate with us, but with the Spirit, and so our lives testify of God.

Just as jars of clay are, we may be battered and bruised in life. We may even shatter! But the treasure that is within is unbreakable. No matter what happens, we are not crushed, we do not despair, and we are never abandoned. What God has fashioned and redeemed cannot be destroyed.

Although at times I am struck down, your power, Lord, preserves me. I have an unwavering strength within me that attests to your presence with me. Thank you for saving me from death and sending me your Holy Spirit.

Are you living as one who is indestructible?

BELIEVE IN FAITH

Without faith it is impossible to please God, because anyone who comes to him must believe that he exists and that he rewards those who earnestly seek him.

HEBREWS 11:6 NIV

To truly follow God is not simply to uphold our end of an agreement. We are not bound to obedience out of some obligation or threat. Real faith overflows into our behavior and it becomes a joy to follow our Lord. The only place we want to be is with him because we love him.

If faith is not part of our lives, no amount of moral dealings will please God. He is looking for an active and loving relationship with us, not a robotic and reluctant religious adherence.

You are my greatest reward, Lord God, and you continue to reward me now and store up rewards for me in eternity. How generous you are! I follow you devoutly because I love you with all my heart.

What is the difference between blind faith and coming before God with the sort of faith being spoken of in this verse?

SEEK GOD

The LORD has looked down from heaven
upon the sons of men
to see if there are any who understand,
who seek after God.
PSALM 14:2 NASB

The Lord created us with a yearning to be understood and sought after. He has this same desire and fashioned us in like manner. He loves it when we pursue him and take the time to understand his heart.

Just as we feel blessed when someone remembers what we said, considers what is important to us, and enjoys being around us, so the Lord is honored when we treat him this way. He searches the earth for those whose hearts long for him.

Oh Father, you have loved me intimately and designed me intricately. It is so amazing to be known by you. You see my good and my bad and you pursue me still. I love you as well and deeply desire closeness with you. Every day I will seek to know you more and love you back.

What will you do today to seek after God and understand him better?

THINGS ABOVE

Set your mind on the things above, not on the things that are on earth. For you have died and your life is hidden with Christ in God. When Christ, who is our life, is revealed, then you also will be revealed with Him in glory.

COLOSSIANS 3:2-4 NASB

Paul is not instructing the Colossae believers to ignore their responsibilities or overlook important earthly matters, but in the context of this passage, he is reminding Christians that the goal of our lives is not here in this world.

We exist for God and our lives are found in him. Although we have daily tasks as well as ambitions and goals, we should not lose sight of what really matters and the only things that will last. We are wasted for this world because we live for eternity.

My mind is set on you, Father. I turn to you for wisdom and direction since the ways of this world fall short. You give meaning to my life and motivation to my days. My heart searches for you and finds contentment in you alone.

What are some examples of things on the earth which try to distract you from focusing on things that really matter?

REPENTANCE

*Do you think lightly of the riches of His kindness
and tolerance and patience, not knowing that
the kindness of God leads you to repentance?*

ROMANS 2:4 NASB

As humans, we sometimes wrongly judge sin on a scale.
God does not view iniquity this way, however, since any
imperfection separates us from a perfect God. We should
refrain from comparing sin, judging others, or devaluing the
grace that has been shown to us.

There is nobody who God's grace cannot extend to, if they
would just be willing to receive it. As Christians, we should
adamantly admit our need for God's grace and be willing
to extend grace to others, regardless of how we weigh and
measure their sin.

**Lord, may I never underestimate the atrocity of my sin
or the greatness of your kindness. Of far greater value is
your patience toward me, dear God, than all the riches of
this world. Thank you for leading me to repentance and
forgiving all my sin.**

How did God's kindness lead you to repentance?

COUNSEL

Without counsel plans fail,
but with many advisers they succeed.
PROVERBS 15:22 ESV

Each of us bear God's image, but none of us bear his whole image. He created us differently so we could learn to work together. Everyone has different strengths and different vantage points, so we need each other to thrive in life. If we were to attempt life by our own strength alone, we would suffer greatly and have many upsets.

By inviting others into our life and plans, and staying open and humble to receive critique, we set ourselves up for victory. Seeking the counsel of others is paramount to success. Intentionally inquiring of others who think differently than us helps reveal a lot that we may have not otherwise considered.

You are the great counselor, Lord God. Without your guidance, I would be lost. Please soften my heart to also invite the involvement of others into my decision making and dilemmas. When I reach an impasse, I will turn to you and to those you have given me for help and advice.

Who do you go to for counsel and advice?

ENDURING TEMPTATION

The temptations in your life are no different from what others experience. And God is faithful. He will not allow the temptation to be more than you can stand. When you are tempted, he will show you a way out so that you can endure.

1 CORINTHIANS 10:13 NLT

Salvation does not exclude us from worldly consequences. We are given salvation freely, but then instructed to behave a certain way.

God's commandments are out of love, and he always provides a way through the most difficult of times. Like a good Father, he guides us through and guards us from enduring too much. Although at times it may feel like too much for us, it is not too much for him.

In my bleakest moments, Father God, your loving embrace is that much more welcomed. Instead of caving to temptation, I will fall on you. Never will you let me go or fail me. You are always faithful. I trust you wholeheartedly.

Do you believe that you can overcome any temptation with God's help?

PASSIONATE LOVE

Listen to me all you godly ones:
Love the Lord with passion!
The Lord protects and preserves all those who are loyal to him.
But he pays back in full all those who reject him in their pride.
PSALM 31:23 TPT

The Lord has shown himself to be willing to suffer many of our vices, but he cannot protect and preserve someone who outright refuses to accept it. Those who are lost to pride attempt to find their way in their own strength. They do not admit they need God's saving grace, and therefore turn down his gift.

Those who are humble, who see their failings and limitations, and who recognize their need for a Savior are invited to accept God's free gift. He will protect these people and preserve them always. He will be loyal forever to those who chose loyalty to him.

Your passionate love encompasses me, dear Lord, and I cannot turn my back on you. You are my protection and the one who holds my life in your hands. I cannot navigate this life without you and I thank you for showing me the way home. I am your beloved child forever.

In what ways can you passionately love God?

GENTLENESS

"Blessed are the gentle, for they shall inherit the earth."
MATTHEW 5:5 NASB

The word gentle used in this verse is also often translated as meek. The Greek word for meekness referred to a war horse that had been tamed. Only the very best horses who were highly akin to their rider's voice and who would listen to his commands even in the heat of battle, were used out on the field. The other horses were used to pull cargo and such.

Gentleness and meekness can be inaccurately understood as weakness. Being gentle before God and attentive to his voice takes focus and discipline. It takes practice, training, humility, and patience. True gentleness is of great value to a believer, and there is nothing weak about it.

Lord, I want to be used by you and hear your voice. Teach me to be gentle and to focus on your voice instead of becoming overwhelmed by the battles around me.

Why would God choose to entrust the earth to the gentle and meek?

COMPASSION AND JUSTICE

The LORD longs to be gracious to you;
therefore he will rise up to show you compassion.
For the LORD is a God of justice.
Blessed are all who wait for him!

ISAIAH 30:18 NIV

The beautiful blending of God's compassion and justice is what gives us the hope that he will amend everything in his timing. We long for his justice now, but he compassionately holds back his judgment a while longer.

This same compassion forgave our sins and showed us grace when we were worthy of death. God's amazing grace lifts us back up. We wait patiently for the Lord because we know his grace is abounding and his fairness is exact.

What an incredible gift your compassion is, Father. Before I ever pray for judgment on anyone, please remind me of the compassion you have shown me. You truly are a just God, and you enact your judgment when it is time. I do not know the time, but you do. I trust you fully and wait patiently for you.

How has God shown you grace?

GIVING THANKS

Everything God created is good,
and nothing is to be rejected
if it is received with thanksgiving.

1 TIMOTHY 4:4 NIV

At the time when Paul wrote this letter to Timothy, there was an ungodly practice rising in popularity called "asceticism." It taught that spiritualism could be obtained through rejecting worldly comforts since anything of the physical realm was corrupt. Paul pointed out that although pleasurable things such as food, wine, or sex could be over indulged in and become gluttony, alcoholism, or lust, God still created each of them for our pleasure.

We do have to be careful though. If someone is struggling with lack, overcoming unhealthy habits, or their conscience is still disturbed, then we need to prioritize them over our own pleasurable partaking to show love and consideration.

God, with gladness I give thanks to you for everything you have given me to enjoy. You love to see me happy, and nothing makes me happier than you do.

How do you give thanks to God for his wonderful gifts?

MARCH

Let us then with confidence
draw near to the throne of grace,
that we may receive mercy and find
grace to help in time of need.

HEBREWS 4:16 ESV

FAITHFUL SERVICE

Only fear the Lord and serve him faithfully with all your heart.
For consider what great things he has done for you.
1 SAMUEL 12:24 ESV

Our obedience to God is not conditional for salvation. Rather, it is in response to our salvation. His saving grace is given freely to those who follow him. By faithfully serving him, we demonstrate how grateful we are for our redemption and how much we love him.

We fear the Lord by reverently respecting him, his position, and his power. He does not want us cowering in a corner or attempting to hide our sins. He invites us to approach him and let him carry our burdens. Proper fear of the Lord should compel us to continue in obedience and not to run away from his loving embrace.

When considering all the great things you have done for me, Almighty God, I become overwhelmed by your goodness and your power. I want to demonstrate my love and devotion to you, so I obey your leadership with joy in my heart. In faith, I will continue to serve you and praise your name.

How has the Lord asked you to faithfully serve him?

GENUINE AFFECTION

Love each other with genuine affection,
and take delight in honoring each other.
ROMANS 12:10 NLT

Since we are of the same body and members of God's family, we should love other believers as if they were our literal brothers and sisters. In fact, the genuine love Paul is talking about comes from the Greek word philia which is where the name Philadelphia came from, the city of brotherly love.

Rather than seeking our own glory, we should be delighted when someone else receives honor. Our love should be familial and not self-seeking. Even when siblings fight, there is a loyalty and a love that exists within a healthy family that cannot be undone by strife.

Thank you for grafting me into your family, dear Lord. Thank you for the love you show me and the love that you've woven throughout your family of followers.

If all believers gave preference to each other, what would it look like to the world?

TRUSTWORTHINESS

A gossip betrays a confidence,
but a trustworthy person keeps a secret.
PROVERBS 11:13 NIV

When someone confides in us, to break that confidence is a breach of trust. There are always exceptions when safety is in question, but if the motive of our hearts is self-centered, it is a telling sign that we should remain quiet. The secrets of others are never meant as a tool to further our own reputations.

Our character before the Lord should matter to us far more than our standings with others. We ought to strive to be people of trustworthiness and discretion. Others should feel safe and cared for when they willingly share their hearts with us.

You are a safe and inviting place for me to run to, Father, and I long to be that for others as well. Anytime I am tempted to use information that belongs to someone else to make myself seem more important, please remind me of this verse and help me stay quiet. May I never speak poorly of others behind their back but address matters discreetly and lovingly.

Would you consider yourself trustworthy with information told to you in confidence?

PRESSING HEAVENWARD

One thing I do: Forgetting what is behind and straining toward what is ahead, I press on toward the goal to win the prize for which God has called me heavenward in Christ Jesus.
PHILIPPIANS 3:13-14 NIV

Maturity is not something which accidentally happens in the life of a believer. If we want to grow in faith and in the knowledge of God, we have to press on toward those goals. Like a runner who is racing to win, so should the motivation of being called by God stir up a passion in us that we strain forward with a single focus.

Furthermore, if we are focused on what is behind or beside us, we will lose our direction and speed. Keeping our eyes on Christ guarantees our place in the race.

Lord, as I press on heavenward, sometimes the road seems long and wearisome. Please refresh me and remind me of how worth it you truly are.

Have you held yourself back because of past mistakes, or are you able to forget what is behind and truly run toward God?

PATH OF LIFE

You make known to me the path of life;
you will fill me with joy in your presence,
with eternal pleasures at your right hand.
PSALM 16:11 NIV

The path to life can be treacherous at times. It often leads us places we do not like to go. However, there is joy found in the journey. Not only are there eternal pleasures stored up for those who remain faithful, but there are rewards here now for following God. The greatest of these rewards is that we grow closer to God the more we walk with him. We understand his love, his character, and his plan better because we have a relationship with him.

Following God is the only path that leads to true and lasting life. When we stay the course, he fills us with joy, makes his presence known, and leads us every step of the way.

Lord, you have made known to me the path of life, and now I ask that you help me walk in it. Your presence fills me with joy, and my deepest desire is simply to be with you. Please continue to walk with me.

What sort of eternal pleasures has God promised to those who faithfully follow him?

CALLOUSED HEARTS

"This people's heart has become calloused; they hardly hear with their ears, and they have closed their eyes. Otherwise they might see with their eyes, hear with their ears, understand with their hearts and turn, and I would heal them."
MATTHEW 13:15 NIV

Although the Scriptures often use sickness and sin synonymously, the term heal in this context, concurs with the idea of pardoning or turning them back. Far more important than our physical healing is our spiritual condition before God.

To become calloused usually takes time of repeated motions. If we're simply performing the act of Christianity without investing in our relationship with Christ, we will grow calloused. Or if we're mimicking the ways of the world, that will eventually harden our hearts as well. God's warning is clear: open our hearts, ears, and eyes so we can understand and find healing for our souls.

God, please do not allow my heart to grow hard. The devil tries to lull me into a false sense of security, to make me believe I do not need to stand guard. Wake me up, God! I do not want to spiritually sleep, so light the fire in me again, I pray.

What keeps you awake and alert to the spiritual war you are engaged in?

WALKING BLAMELESS

The one whose walk is blameless is kept safe,
but the one whose ways are perverse will fall into the pit.

PROVERBS 28:18 NIV

When we tinker with sin, it gets a hold of us and drags us off course. We cannot serve both God and ourselves; either we are walking his path which leads to life, or we are walking a path we forged ourselves which will ultimately get us lost.

The Lord is a patient guide who knows how to safely lead us around snares. We, however, only have a human perspective and cannot see the pits that lay around us. Although we fall, we may once again call out to God and he will lift us out of the pit. There is a final pit, however, for those who obstinately refuse to accept God's hand.

Help me walk blamelessly, Lord, by leading me forward and guiding my steps. Although my own eyes may deceive me, you will never forsake me. I find safety in you alone, for you are gracious and kind.

What does it mean to walk blamelessly?

QUICK TO LISTEN

Understand this, my dear brothers and sisters:
You must all be quick to listen,
slow to speak, and slow to get angry.
JAMES 1:19 NLT

Learning to walk in a manner worthy of being called children of God means that we adjust our behavior and actions accordingly. When we project ourselves above others, rattle off impromptu responses, fail to respect others enough to listen, and are easily set off, we demonstrate self-love not self-control.

A child of God learns how to be humble, patient, considerate, wise, and controlled. Even God listens to us, waits until the time is right to speak, and holds back his righteous anger. We have been given the opportunity to exhibit the same characteristics.

Lord, teach me how to be self-controlled. Rather than giving in to the whims of my emotions, please fill my heart with peace.

There are times when you should speak and feel angry, but not be hasty or careless. How can you stop yourself from responding to a situation in anger?

GOD HEARS US

Since we know he hears us when we make our requests,
we also know that he will give us what we ask for.

1 JOHN 5:15 NLT

The purpose of prayer is not to simply submit our list of requests to God. Prayer was designed so we could have communion with God and grow in our relationship with him. Through prayer, we can better understand and be involved in the will of God. If we ask God for something and our request is not granted, then we know it was not part of his divine plan.

Ultimately, it is his will that we want and pray for. Therefore, if we go before God in prayer, submitting ourselves to his will and asking that he align our hearts with his, we know that whatever we ask will be granted because he wants our participation in his masterful plan.

Teach me your will, Lord, and use me. I deeply desire to know you more and walk closer with you. I want to be used by you for your glory. This is what I ask for. This is what I know you will grant.

How can you know that you are praying for something within God's will?

INSTRUCTION

I will instruct you and teach you in the way you should go;
I will counsel you with my loving eye on you.
PSALM 32:8 NIV

God is not a harsh general who issues his soldiers marching orders and sends them off to war alone. In love, he is constantly training us how to act, equipping us with everything we need for victory, and showing us the way to go. In fact, he goes before us and shields us from danger. He is never far off nor disinterested.

God's eye is continually on us like a watchful parent, and his counsel is always available. Wise children will receive his teaching and instruction, they will seek out his counsel, and they will not be afraid because they know who their Father is.

God, you are a good teacher, and I soak up your lessons. Your patience reassures me and your presence strengthens me. There is no hardship that I cannot face with you by my side. You have already given me everything I need to succeed.

How do you receive counsel from the Lord? How does he instruct you?

RIGHTEOUS SHOWERS

Sow righteousness for yourselves,
reap the fruit of unfailing love,
and break up your unplowed ground;
for it is time to seek the LORD,
until he comes and showers his righteousness on you.

HOSEA 10:12 NIV

The Israelites had walked away from God. They disregarded all the goodness he had shown them and praised themselves for their own accomplishments. Their hearts had grown hard like unplowed ground. There was no fruit in their lives.

The Lord continued to pursue them just like he does with us when we are unfaithful to him. He sent the prophet Hosea to remind the Israelites of how much he loved them and of all the blessings he had given them. If only they would open their hearts and choose to live righteously again, he would shower his grace and righteousness on them. There is no better time than now to return to the one who loves us the most.

Forgive me for my unfaithfulness, Father God, for I often lose sight and follow my own path. I fail to attribute my successes and blessings to you and my heart forgets your words. You are so ready to welcome me back and accept me as your own. Please shower on me your righteousness today.

What is the fruit of God's unfailing love that he has given to you?

THANKS ALWAYS

Giving thanks always for all things unto God and the Father in the name of our Lord Jesus Christ.

EPHESIANS 5:20 KJV

Paul had been instructing the Ephesian believers to be "filled with the Spirit" (v 18). This is a continuation of the description of what that would look like in the life of a Christian. When we live for Christ and dwell on him, we become increasingly aware of all he has done for us. This, in turn, leads to gratitude.

When we have a grateful perspective on life, the injustices inflicted on us grow dim in comparison. We have been forgiven of all our sins and granted eternal life. We have a personal relationship with a loving God who is always faithful and always nearby.

Dear Lord, although I endure wounds and wrongdoings throughout my life, help me choose to dwell instead on everything you have done for me. Evil cannot steal my joy. Losses cannot distract me from the thankfulness I have for you. My perspective is eternal and so is my gratitude.

How would it impact your life if you had a grateful spirit throughout your day?

CONSTRUCTIVE CRITICISM

If you listen to constructive criticism,
you will be at home among the wise.
If you reject discipline, you only harm yourself;
but if you listen to correction, you grow in understanding.
PROVERBS 15:31-32 NLT

Most of us do not enjoy our flaws being pointed out, but if we can learn to appreciate it then we can begin the hard work of growing and maturing. A truly loving person will offer constructive criticism in a kind way rather than allow us to continue harmful or foolish behavior. By rejecting their help, we only hurt ourselves and a relationship with one who truly cares.

Wisdom comes to those who walk humbly. By admitting our faults and addressing our weaknesses, we can grow in understanding and become more like Christ.

God, I want to grow in wisdom more than I want to protect my ego. Please help me to proactively listen when someone is trying to help me because people who are loving enough to offer correction are a blessing from you. Teach me how to listen, how to learn, and how to love in return.

How well do you receive criticism? Do you push it away, deny its usefulness, or learn from it and grow?

LOVE COVERS

Above all, love each other deeply,
because love covers over a multitude of sins.

1 PETER 4:8 NIV

Love is what sets us apart from the world. We identify with Jesus because of love. Often love is not earned or deserved; it is given. Love can be very difficult and require all our strength. In fact, the type of love Peter is defining here as deep comes from the Greek word ektene, which was a term used to define an athlete's muscles when they were being strained to win a race. With this same determination, we are to love each other deeply above all else.

When we love others deeply, there is no room for sin to fester and cause bitterness. We can forgive sins, focus forward, mend relationships, and leave injustice in the capable hands of Christ. This is not easy, but with love it is possible.

Jesus, the love you showed me stands as a direct contrast to the love media and the world tries to sell. Please help me to truly love others with all my might. I do not want my love to be tainted by sin, so I will choose to cover sin with love.

Is there someone in your life you are striving to love?
Is unforgiveness or bitterness impeding you?

HEART MEDITATIONS

*Let the words of my mouth
and the meditation of my heart
be acceptable to you,
O LORD, my rock and my redeemer.*

PSALM 19:14 ESV

Honoring God both with what we think and what we say is the only acceptable way to live. Only God can see the condition of our hearts, and if our words are masking the sin we have allowed to seep in, what does it actually benefit us? We must first address what is in our hearts, and from that our words will flow.

Speaking truth and words which are edifying can also help to guide our hearts back to where they ought to be if our hearts are willing to be guided. So, even if kindness and goodness is not how our hearts feel, by insisting that our speech is pure, our hearts can begin to change.

In you, I find redemption and a reliable foundation, Father God. I pray that the meditations hidden away in my heart as well as the words which proceed from my mouth are both pleasing and acceptable to you.

Why are the secret places of your heart as well as the publicity of your words both important to the Lord?

ASK AND RECEIVE

"Until now you have asked nothing in my name.
Ask, and you will receive, that your joy may be full."
JOHN 16:24 ESV

The disciples had obviously asked God for many things before Jesus uttered these words. However, Jesus had been with them on earth. He had not yet accomplished on the cross what he came to earth to do, he had not stood as mediator before God for us, the veil had not yet been torn, and the Holy Spirit had not been given to us.

Christ's death and resurrection provided the way for us to approach God once again because our sins had been forgiven. The Holy Spirit came to help guide us in the way we should go, and he reforms our minds to be one with Christ. When we pray and our hearts are aligned with what that of Jesus, God will surely give us everything we need and fill our joy.

It is only by your grace, Lord Jesus, that I can approach God in prayer and ask for what is holy. Please continue to transform my mind to be more like yours. Thank you for filling me with joy!

What does it mean to ask in Jesus' name?

UNFATHOMABLE

Do you not know? Have you not heard?
The Lord is the everlasting God,
the Creator of the ends of the earth.
He will not grow tired or weary,
and his understanding no one can fathom.

ISAIAH 40:28 NIV

Unlike us, the Lord never grows weary of doing good, not does he tire of loving us and acting lovingly toward us. He is the Creator of the universe, and he diligently upholds the world, governs it wisely, and judges it righteously. With vigor and strength, he provides for all his creation, from the birds to the grass to his beloved Church.

With an unfathomable understanding and infinite love that none of us could begin to grasp, he cares for all our needs out of his goodness. He understands each of us, considers our desires, and gives us all a unique calling.

Lord, you are majestic and all your ways are perfect! You have crafted everything I know with care and consideration. Your eyes are always on me, and you lead me in the path of righteousness. In all this, you never grow weary. You are so good.

How is it different serving a God who understands than a god who is distant?

DO GOOD

Therefore, whenever we have the opportunity, we should do good to everyone—especially to those in the family of faith.
GALATIANS 6:10 NLT

As Christians and members of God's worldwide family, we cannot become so engrossed in our own lives that we miss out on opportunities to help others—especially other believers since we are in the same family. We are not called to lead individual, disconnected lives. Community and fellowship are aspects of faith that God designed for us to engage in.

Some ways Paul teaches us that we can do good to others is by gently restoring someone trapped in sin and carrying each other's burdens. Sin is messy and we tend to like to avoid anything associated with it. Yet when we examine the life of Christ, we see that he constantly communed with sinners, gently pointed them toward the truth, and bore the weight of their sin on his own shoulders.

Oh God, may I not be so set on keeping my life so pristine and unafflicted that I miss out on opportunities that you have laid before me to love others and do good. May I run to sinners and bear their burdens with them because that is exactly what you did for me.

What opportunities are available for you today to do good?

CONFIDENT TRUST

Do not throw away this confident trust in the Lord.
Remember the great reward it brings you!
HEBREWS 10:35 NLT

After an entire book dedicated to validating and strengthening a Christian's confidence in Christ, this warning is issued: do not lose it. Maintain your confidence and trust in God. In the end, it will be rewarded.

The best way to remain confident is by remembering the truths of the Gospel. We must immerse ourselves regularly in the Word so the subtle lies and twisting of truth that the world constantly bombards us with do not begin to corrupt our confidence.

Help us to hold fast, Father. Give us wisdom to discern truth from the lies and to confidently stand on faith in you alone. We are confident that you are the only way, and we reject anything that tries to dismantle our assurance.

Do you surround yourself with truth? What sort of messages are you being told daily?

WAIT PATIENTLY

Be still before the Lᴏʀᴅ and wait patiently for him;
do not fret when people succeed in their ways,
when they carry out their wicked schemes.

Pꜱᴀʟᴍ 37:7 ɴɪᴠ

It can be difficult to watch the wicked succeed in their ways, but we know that God is also aware of their choices. When the actions of selfish people negatively impact us, we can become angry and desire to issue our own form of justice. In these moments, it is important that we remember not to let our anger lead us to sin.

God is the judge of all things. Our interference only exacerbates the situation. Instead of lashing out, we ought to continue to insist on doing what is right, trust God, and wait patiently for him to vindicate all actions. His timing is perfect.

Father, forgive me for when I attempt to assume your role as judge. I am not as capable, as wise, or as loving as you. Please give me patience to allow you to address wickedness as I continue to pursue the way of grace and holiness.

Why is it so hard to wait patiently when you know that God is just?

DEVOTED TO PRAYER

Devote yourselves to prayer,
keeping alert in it with an attitude of thanksgiving.
COLOSSIANS 4:2 NASB

Prayer was not meant to be simply an act of obedience or an event. It is a dialogue, an ongoing conversation. God in not far off or uninterested; he desires to be involved in our lives and to have an ongoing relationship with us. Prayer and thanksgiving go hand in hand because the more we pray and draw close to God, the more aware we become of his abounding love and care for us. A person devoted to praying who is truly listening for God's responses will be a thankful person.

Prayer should also not be carefree, but intentional. By keeping alert in it, we recognize that there are many obstacles which we must guard ourselves against. Prayer keeps us not only vigilant but connected to God who is our source of strength.

Lord, thank you for tearing down the barrier between me and you. I am so grateful to be permitted access to you through prayer, and I will not regard this gift lightly. I devote myself to you, to prayer, and to listening for your responses.

What does a deliberate and devoted prayer life do for you?

HARMONY

*Let us aim for harmony in the church
and try to build each other up.*
ROMANS 14:19 NLT

We have been given incredible freedom in Christ, but we should also make every effort to not abuse this freedom. Just because we will be forgiven does not mean we should proceed to sin. Likewise, simply because we are allowed to eat or do certain things, it does not give us the right to judge others. The Lord alone is Judge, so we should refrain from creating unnecessary conflict at the expense of others.

When peace can prevail, Paul says this is what we should choose. At times, that may mean setting aside our rights for the sake of harmony with someone else. When those instances come up, we should see it as an opportunity to love and serve Christ.

Jesus, you are the Prince of Peace and it is my honor to emulate you through the way I live. I can let go of petty disagreements and navigate through upsetting conflict because your peace unites me with others and because you are worth it.

Are your rights and freedoms of more value to you than peace and harmony?

VICTORY

Where there is no guidance the people fall,
but in abundance of counselors there is victory.
PROVERBS 11:14 NASB

By surrounding ourselves with other godly, wise people, our chances of success increase exponentially. None of us can see all sides and inviting others to play an active part in our lives guarantees a broader vision. Others can offer warning, counsel, encouragement, and correction—all of which are vital for spiritual growth.

The Lord has given us a body of believers intentionally so we can learn to work and play together. When we cut ourselves off from other believers and attempt to navigate this world on our own, we are far more likely to fall, and there will be nobody to help us back up. God created us for fellowship and community.

God, in your great understanding, you created me to need others. In my pride, I often attempt to carry my burden alone and find my own way. Please help me to humbly accept the help and counsel of others, and to seek out guidance when I need it.

What is the best way to ensure victory for yourself and others?

LOVE OTHERS

If I had the gift of prophecy, and if I understood all of God's secret plans and possessed all knowledge, and if I had such faith that I could move mountains, but didn't love others, I would be nothing. If I gave everything I have to the poor and even sacrificed my body, I could boast about it; but if I didn't love others, I would have gained nothing.

1 CORINTHIANS 13:2-4 NLT

There is such a tendency within the Church to become so focused on the gifts of the Spirit, that we overlook the necessity for the fruit of the Spirit. The very first fruit mentioned is love. While the Corinthian Christians were comparing gifts with one another, elevating some over others, and using them for their own gain and fame, Paul stepped in to remind them that their focus should be on love.

We are each given gifts to use, for the love of God and for the service of others. Even worse than missing the greater cause, Paul warned believers that if they exercise their gifts without love, they actually accomplish nothing.

Lord, rather than wasting my gifts on pointless pursuits like my own aggrandizement, I want to hold a position of surrender to you and to your better discernment. Fill me with your love, Lord Jesus.

What gifts have you been given and how can you put them to use in love?

BLESSED

You make him most blessed forever;
you make him glad with the joy of your presence.
PSALM 21:6 ESV

In writing about King David, the psalmist declared that it is the Lord who has blessed him. First, David's worldly riches could be attributed to God placing him in his position as king, and second, the Lord's blessings far outweigh all of the earth's treasures. David was allotted both.

David was blessed forever because of his faith in the Lord which leads to eternal life, but also because from his lineage the Messiah would be born—so his line continues forever. The psalmist made it clear that David's joy was not from his position as king or all the glory he had accumulated on the earth. Rather, his joy came from being in the presence of the Lord.

Oh Lord, you so richly bless me, and still the sweetest gift is my relationship with you. Regardless of whether I am royalty or utterly destitute, my joy comes from being with you and spending time in your presence.

Have you spent time in the presence of the Lord lately?

BELIEVE

Overhearing what they said, Jesus told him,
"Don't be afraid; just believe."
MARK 5:36 NIV

Jairus had just received news that his twelve-year-old daughter had been proclaimed dead. What incredible pain and fear that must have tortured him with. Jesus, however, overheard the news and encouraged him with such a simple but profound statement: "Don't be afraid; just believe."

When we encounter death or loss, do we approach it with faith? Maybe we will not experience a loved one being raised from the dead in this life, but one day we will! Remember, Jesus Christ has already overcome death, and its rule is temporary. There will come a day when the dead in Christ will be raised from the dead, so we do not need to fear. We only need to believe the words of the one who holds all power over life and death!

Oh Father, sometimes death can be so frightening that it paralyzes me. It may be the fear of my own death or other loved ones, or the unjust and rampant killing of innocent strangers I never knew. Whomever it may be, you are still the King in control! I am in your hands and death does not control my faith.

How did Jairus' faith influence the outcome of Jesus' miracle?

SET APART

"Before I formed you in the womb I knew you,
before you were born I set you apart."

JEREMIAH 1:5 NIV

Nobody was an accident or an afterthought. The Lord has carefully crafted every person uniquely. He loved each of us before we were even born because he planned in his heart and mind exactly how we were meant to be.

Sometimes we try to deviate away from how the Lord created us and the calling he has placed on our lives, but as we search for peace to accept who we are and how we were formed, we can have confidence that the Lord truly knows us. He knew us before the world began to hurt and influence us, and he knows how to restore us as well.

Father God, you have set me apart as a unique and dearly loved masterpiece. Thank you for creating me the way you did. I want to give you all the glory for my life. Whenever I am confused or envious of someone else, please remind me to focus on you and allow you to show me why you made me the way you did.

How are you set apart?

SPIRIT OF POWER

God gave us a spirit not of fear
but of power and love and self-control.
2 TIMOTHY 1:7 ESV

Timothy had served alongside Paul for quite a while, and 1 Cor 16:10 suggests that he may have preferred to work that way since he was struggling with fear and being intimidated. Here, Paul, the outspoken and gregarious leader, wrote to Timothy to remind him that it is God who puts a spirit of power and self-control in him. He has nothing to fear since he is engaged in the Lord's work.

We are also given a spirit of power, love, and self-control, so we need not fear when God calls us to a specific work. We can rely on him to help us stand and do exactly what he wants us to.

Help me to be brave, Father God. When I am intimidated or want to hide in the shadows, please remind me that it is you who works in and through me. I do not have a spirit of fear, for the Spirit of God lives in me, filling me with power and self-control.

What intimidates you? Has God asked you to step up or speak up?

STAY CALM

The Lord himself will fight for you. Just stay calm.

EXODUS 14:14 NLT

The Israelites saw God's miracles and followed him through Moses to freedom. Yet, their past captors pursued them. They found themselves cornered and surrounded. Their enemy, determined to destroy them or drag them back into captivity, appeared so mighty. They felt unmatched and hopeless, and so lost faith in the Lord.

Moses reminded the people that it is the Lord who fights for them, as is always the case with the people of God. We may be no match for our enemies, but they are no match for God. When our bondages seem too tight, or our pasts threaten to drag us back down, or when it seems like an impenetrable force is all around us refusing to let us move forward, we need to turn to God. Stand your ground, stay calm, and watch God work on your behalf.

Help me not get so caught up in my own weaknesses or the strength of my enemies that I forget who you are. You are the God who freed me from bondage, forgave my past, led me to life and freedom, and have given me the victory. None can stand against you.

How have you seen the Lord fight for you?

THE LITTLE

Better is the little of the righteous
than the abundance of many wicked.

PSALM 37:16 NASB

The abundance of the wicked may be tantalizing to those of us who have very little, but the little that the righteous have is of far greater value. To gain wealth through evil means is worthless because the days of the wicked are numbered.

Whether the Lord has blessed us with great wealth or taught us to endure with very little, we are to offer what we have to God and find contentment in him alone. This life and its treasures will pass away, so the Lord seeks to increase our faith. All the pleasures of this life pale in comparison to a life lived serving the Lord, for true joy is found in him alone.

Father, worldly wealth does not entice me. You alone are my reward and eternal provision. I praise you for an inheritance that will endure forever. Whether you choose to give me much or little in this life, I will honor you with it and live for you alone.

How can you choose to be happy with the little you have?

EXTRAVAGANT GRACE

*You have experienced the extravagant grace of our
Lord Jesus Christ, that although he was infinitely rich,
he impoverished himself for our sake, so that by his poverty,
we could become rich beyond measure.*

2 CORINTHIANS 8:9 TPT

Jesus taught us what it looks like to put the needs of others before our own. We were deserving of death and he held all riches in his hand, yet he left heaven to die on our behalf. In exchange, we were given an inheritance that will never pass away and have secured a spot in heaven.

When we are treated unjustly by others, we need to have a perspective that is bigger than simply what is fair. Rather than try to get even, we should consider what our fate would have been if Jesus had not intervened on our behalf.

Your extravagant grace, Jesus, has saved my soul from hell. The way you ask me to show you my gratitude is by how I treat other people. It does not matter if they are deserving or if all things are fair, I will love others because I love you. I love you because you first loved me.

Who will you love today? How?

APRIL

He gives grace generously.
As the Scriptures say,
"God opposes the proud
but gives grace to the humble."

JAMES 4:6 NLT

SHIELD OF SALVATION

You have also given me the shield of Your salvation;
Your gentleness has made me great.
2 SAMUEL 22:36 NKJV

This verse was part of a song that David sang to God when he delivered him from Saul's attempts to murder him. Its truth is resounding and it is recorded again in Psalm 18:35. We ought to praise God for his protection when it happens and give all the glory to him.

Simply because we follow God does not mean we will not encounter enemies or have trouble. We will most likely be confronted with all sorts of perilous forces, yet God sustains us. Even if we were to be struck down, our ultimate shield is that we have been given salvation in Christ. Nothing can destroy us because our lives are preserved in Jesus.

God, thank you for being my shield of salvation. You guard me from my enemies, including my ultimate enemy: death. The devil may wound me, but you always preserve me. In your gentleness you have forgiven my sin and made me great.

How does God's meekness make you great?

ASSOCIATION

Live in harmony with one another. Do not be proud, but be willing to associate with people of low position. Do not be conceited.
ROMANS 12:16 NIV

There are times when it is wonderful to search a matter out, and other times when matters should be set aside for the sake of unity and harmony. Paul is not commanding us all to replicate each other or think exactly alike, in fact he predicts the impossibility of this in Romans 14. What he is requiring is that we learn to adjust ourselves and our lives to live harmoniously with others.

Within an orchestra, all instruments play a different piece, but they collaborate to produce beautiful and harmonious music. We can be our own unique selves without arrogantly insisting on our own way and clashing with others around us.

Lord, I recognize that you creatively and majestically designed everyone differently, so that your wonderous personality could be proclaimed vividly throughout the earth. Please teach me to live in harmony with others, including those whose views differ from my own.

Why will pride and conceit keep you from living synchronized with others?

LET IT GO

Starting a quarrel is like breaching a dam;
so drop the matter before a dispute breaks out.
PROVERBS 17:14 NIV

Why should we intentionally invite trouble? There is a godly, biblical way to dispute matters that holds to the intention of ultimately reaching a peaceful resolution. By picking a fight, we fail to honor God, love others, and pursue peace. When we act in a way that is contrary to God's character, we are not honoring him or behaving like his witnesses.

When we pick a fight with someone, we welcome a flood of problems. God does not tell us we need to always be right. He does tell us to honor one another and to live peacefully when it is at all possible.

Reign in my heart, Lord God, and fill me with peace. I want to properly represent you and the peace that you bring, but if my life is full of quarreling and unrest, how can I say I follow your ways? Help me let go of issues that do not matter and cling to your Word as my guiding light.

Do you always have to have the last word or prove your point? What would it take for you to honor God by letting things go?

CONTENTMENT

I know what it is to be in need, and I know what it is to have plenty.
I have learned the secret of being content in any and every
situation, whether well fed or hungry, whether living in plenty or in
want. I can do all this through him who gives me strength.
PHILIPPIANS 4:12-13 NIV

Just like Jesus, who lived as a King and a carpenter, a
Savior and a convicted criminal (although innocent), Paul
encourages us from a place of understanding. He had been
a leader and a prisoner, having plenty and having nothing.
Through it all, he echoed the teachings of Christ when he
revealed that our strength and our contentment is found in
God alone.

We are never left helpless because God is constantly
ready to be our help and our defense. Remember not to
find confidence or surety in worldly acclaims or possessions
because these things can vanish in a moment. The peace and
power of God, however, is eternal and guaranteed.

**I will always turn to you for my contentment, dear God,
and not attempt to find it in my position here on earth.
This world will pass away, but your kingdom is eternal.**

What sort of things do you try to find contentment in?
What do you find instead?

MY SHEPHERD

The Lord is my shepherd; I shall not want.
He makes me lie down in green pastures.
He leads me beside still waters.
He restores my soul.
He leads me in paths of righteousness for his name's sake.

PSALM 23:1-3 ESV

As a shepherd himself, David understood the importance of a shepherd in the lives of sheep. Without a shepherd, sheep are vulnerable to all the elements and dangers of the wild. Even finding food and water would be a struggle.

A good shepherd offers protection, refreshment, and direction. David confidently declared that God is like a good shepherd and that we will lack nothing under his watchful care.

God, innately I love to nurture and care for others. I have inherited this from you, my Good Shepherd. Thank you for loving and caring for me, for leading and guiding me, and for giving my weary soul much needed rest.

Have you been hurt by the world? Rather than clinging to your pain, how can you turn to God for restoration of your soul?

WEIGHTINESS

*"By your words you will be justified,
and by your words you will be condemned."*
MATTHEW 12:37 ESV

Our words often betray what is in our hearts. When our hearts are dark, what we say will also be. If we are filled with the joy of Christ, our speech will reflect this. God always hears and considers what we say to others, or even what we say about others. Our words matter to him.

The tongue is likened to a wild fire that can destroy an entire forest (James 3:6). With our words, we can choose to harm others or help them heal. We must be masters of our mouths and not allow them to master us, or else we could be condemned by the hurtful, careless words we inflict on someone else.

May the words I speak edify you always, dear God. Help me learn to bridal my tongue and choose to encourage and love. Teach me to listen and to know when to speak. Jesus, you carefully considered the good it would be before speaking. I want to follow your example.

Why do your words matter so much to God?

TRUSTED WORDS

Better is open rebuke than hidden love.
Wounds from a friend can be trusted,
but an enemy multiplies kisses.
PROVERBS 27:5-6 NIV

With all the self-interest abounding in the world, it can be challenging to discern genuine love. Someone who truly loves like a friend will tell the truth, even if it is unpopular or offensive.

There is good reason to be wary of a person who only flatters and speaks words that they believe will be readily accepted, even at the expense of honesty or what is right. Hold on to genuine friendships and insist on being the sort of friend others can rely on to speak the truth in love.

Lord, your rebuke is welcomed in my life because I know it is delivered in love. You love me enough to not leave me where I am, but to constantly be growing and maturing me. Thank you, Father, even when it hurts.

How can you tell a true friend apart from someone who is self-interested?

LOVE FOR LIFE

Our great desire is that you will keep on loving others as long as life lasts, in order to make certain that what you hope for will come true.

HEBREWS 6:11 NLT

Our salvation is not something we are expected to lay hold of, and then go about our lives in whichever way we desire. Salvation takes what is dead and brings it to life! The way we used to live led to death. The way we are called to live now leads to life.

We are instructed to love others. This is not a suggestion, and it is not easy. It is very, very difficult and yet it is mandated for every believer. The evidence that our life has truly been changed by salvation is recognized in the way we love others.

You are the giver of life, Lord, and I am the grateful recipient. I will not squander your kindness or your gifts but will continue your legacy of love all my days. Even if it is not received or returned, I will insist on taking the hard road of love so that my hope in you will be realized.

What are the dangers of immature or insincere faith?

GOD'S HOME

I heard a loud shout from the throne, saying, "Look, God's home is now among his people! He will live with them, and they will be his people. God himself will be with them. He will wipe every tear from their eyes, and there will be no more death or sorrow or crying or pain. All these things are gone forever."

REVELATION 21:3-4 NLT

Ever since sin entered the world in the Garden of Eden, we have been separated from God. In the Old Testament, he dwelt in the Tabernacle and only the high priest, after performing ceremonious purifying, could approach him. Then, at the crucifixion of Christ, the curtain secluding the temple was torn and believers were invited to approach God in prayer. Still, however, we do not have direct access to God.

On the day we are finally invited into his presence, to live with him forever, we will be rid of all our impurities, everything will be made right, death and sorrow will be ended, and our home will be with him.

How I long for that great day, Lord Jesus! My home is with you and I yearn deeply for your presence.

In what ways has God revealed to you his deep desire to dwell with you? What has hindered that from happening?

TENDER MERCIES

Lord, don't hold back your tender mercies from me.
Let your unfailing love and faithfulness always protect me.
PSALM 40:11 NLT

The Lord loves to bestow his compassion and his kindness on those who ask to receive it. He has so many good things in store for his followers. He never fails to love us, even when we are unloving. His character remains the same, and his promises to us he will surely uphold, even though we have acted disloyally toward him and are unworthy.

God is a good Father and he always protects his children. He wants our engagement because he cares about his relationship with us. We ought to go before him and ask in faith for his goodness and his grace to be upon us.

Lord, thank you for generously giving me so many tender mercies. Whenever I fall, you show me grace again by helping me back up. You never fail to protect me from all the attacks against me because you love me. I praise you, dear Lord, for you are glorious and kind.

Why does God still want you to ask for his mercies even though he loves to give them? How does it benefit you to ask?

STEADFAST LOVE

*The steadfast love of the L*ORD* never ceases;*
his mercies never come to an end;
they are new every morning; great is your faithfulness.
LAMENTATIONS 3:22-23 ESV

God's love is not a one-time gift; it is new every single morning of our lives! He never ceases to pursue us and draw us back to himself. Every day his love for us is full and, forgetting what lies behind, we can run back to him again and again. The mercy he has for us as we stumble after him is limitless. Although we make many mistakes along the way, the Lord only asks that we continue to come to him.

God's faithfulness toward us is great, for he has always remained true to his promises. We are his beloved bride, and he adores us. His faithfulness will never end. His love always endures.

Your steadfast love astounds me, Lord! I seek you every morning for your mercy and grace. All my days are a gift from you, and I thank you for them and for your priceless gifts.

Do your days feel like they all run together? Have you asked God to renew you with his endless love and strength every morning?

COMPASSIONATE

Be kind and compassionate to one another,
forgiving each other, just as in Christ God forgave you.
EPHESIANS 4:32 NIV

It is a well-known prospect that we become like those we associate with. Paul points out earlier in this chapter that traits which define worldly individuals are easily misled, possessing futile thinking, ignorant, hard of heart, insensitive, sensual, indulgent, impure, greedy, bitter, angry, prone to fight, and slanderous.

Instead, we are to be remade in the image of our Maker. He is kind, compassionate, and forgiving. This sort of behavior takes an intentional laying down of self, but it becomes more and more attainable when we spend intentional time with God.

I come before you today and every day, Father, to learn your ways and become more like you. I do not want to be influenced by the world's corrupt patterns, but by your lifegiving characteristics. Make me more like you, Lord.

Why do you think Paul so often writes about the
forgiveness we have received when he is instructing us on
how to treat others?

WISE WORDS

Wise words bring many benefits,
and hard work brings rewards.
PROVERBS 12:14 NLT

To speak wise words, we must be listening to what the Lord is telling us. Wisdom comes from the Lord and we increase in understanding the more we spend time with him and learn from him. When we speak with wise words on behalf of God and not just ourselves, our words bring comfort and encouragement to others. We teach what is true and glorify our Father in heaven.

Although the Lord goes before us to prepare our ways, that does not exempt us from the hard work he has given us to do. Life is laborious and wrought with difficulties. There are rewards for those who dutifully and joyfully work hard as unto the Lord.

Following your leadership, God, I will work hard at the tasks you have given me, without worrying or complaining. Father, please give me your wisdom so that I might receive your benefits and share them with others. I know that your gifts and your wisdom is always for the benefit of the whole body, and I thank you for that.

What benefits might you receive from speaking with wisdom?

INTO MARVELOUS LIGHT

You are a chosen race, a royal priesthood, a holy nation, God's own people, in order that you may proclaim the mighty acts of him who called you out of darkness into his marvelous light.

1 PETER 2:9 NRSV

In ancient Israel, one tribe was chosen to serve as royal priests on behalf of the rest of the tribes: the tribe of Levi. The Israelites were the chosen race and holy nation to testify of God's goodness to the rest of the world. Now, since Jesus Christ removed the barrier between us and God and invited us into his family, we have taken on the mantle of being the royal priesthood.

We can go before God and serve as mediators, praying on behalf of those outside of God's family, and sharing the truth of God's grace with the lost. We are God's chosen people, taken from the darkness and carried into the light.

Lord, thank you for extending your grace to all people. Thank you for calling me out of darkness and into your glorious light. You have grafted me into your family and called me your child.

How do you define your role as a royal priest?

RELIANCE

*I have always been mindful of your unfailing love
and have lived in reliance on your faithfulness.*

PSALM 26:3 NIV

David, in asking for the Lord's vindication, claimed to have lived a blameless life. Clearly David had sinned greatly throughout his life, but his blamelessness came from his reliance on God. Although he had sinned, he trusted in the Lord to convict him, forgive him, and continue to lead him forward.

In everything, David was aware of God's love and knew that God would never fail him. Even though he failed, the Lord's character would remain true. Because David accepted both God's love and his discipline, he knew that he stood blameless before the Lord. No amount of sin can thwart God's faithfulness.

As I learn to fully rely on you, God, I pray that you constantly remind me of your unfailing love. I praise you for your faithfulness and acknowledge my need for your grace and forgiveness.

Are you so reliant on God that you would invite him to search your heart, knowing that you would be found blameless?

TRUE WORSHIPPERS

"A time is coming and has now come when the true worshipers will worship the Father in the Spirit and in truth, for they are the kind of worshipers the Father seeks. God is spirit, and his worshipers must worship in the Spirit and in truth."

JOHN 4:23-24 NIV

The Samaritan women had lived an immoral lifestyle. She was more than simply physically thirsty; she was spiritually thirsty too. She had transitioned from relationship to relationship until becoming an outcast in society. When confronted by Jesus at the well, she asked him where true worshippers ought to worship—fixated on the location. Jesus' response to her in this verse was profound.

It did not matter where geographically she worshipped, so long as it was in spirit and in truth. God saw into her spirit, saw the sin, and desired her anyway. He wanted her to come before him in truth and find forgiveness and love. Furthermore, Jesus offered to vanquish her dryness with his love. She would never need to grow spiritually thirsty again because of his fully satisfying relationship. Her searching was over!

Jesus, your love is everlasting and fills every crevice of my heart. No other relationship satisfies my longing the way you do because my heart was created to love you.

When you feel spiritually dry, do you first try to fill your void with other relationships?

GENTLY LEADING

He tends his flock like a shepherd:
he gathers the lambs in his arms
and carries them close to his heart;
he gently leads those that have young.
ISAIAH 40:11 NIV

Although the Lord is king of the universe and ultimate judge over his creation, he is still the most gentle and loving master that has ever existed.

God leads his people patiently, intentionally fosters a relationship with each of us, provides for all our needs, and comforts us when we are hurting. Like a gentle shepherd, he carries us over obstacles and holds us close to his heart when we are afraid.

I am not a simple number to you, God, for you know me by name. You know me intimately and care deeply for me. I will follow your leadership and praise you for your provisions all the days of my life. Thank you for your comfort when I am hurt and afraid. Thank you for your gentleness toward me as I learn and grow.

How have you seen the gentle leading of the Lord in your life, or felt his comfort when you were hurting?

TIME

Do not forget this one thing, dear friends:
With the Lord a day is like a thousand years,
and a thousand years are like a day.

2 PETER 3:8 NIV

As a rebuttal to the false teachers who claimed that Jesus would not return and there would be no judgement day, Peter reminded his readers that the Lord is not bound to linear time the way we are.

God has a perfect plan in motion, and he tarries because of his great love and mercy. He is patient and kind. However, the judgment day will indeed come, and Christ will come back for his church.

Time seems to tick by just as it always has, but I will not be lulled into a mantra of mediocrity, God. I heed your words and base my life on them. I know you are coming back for me because you have always fulfilled all your promises. You are faithful and true.

How do you feel knowing that God is outside of time?

MATURITY

Solid food is for the mature, who by constant use have trained themselves to distinguish good from evil.
HEBREWS 5:14 NIV

Babies are fed, coddled, and given special baby food. When someone first comes to faith in Christ, they cannot be expected to grasp complex concepts immediately. There is grace for that, for sanctification is a journey. As babies mature into children and eventually adults, however, they are expected to wean off baby food and eat more substantial food.

The same process is true for a Christian. We should not be apathetic or lazy. Through time with God, study of his Word, fellowship with other believers, and the testing of our faith, we mature and should embrace the progression.

Thank you for being patient with me, Father, as I mature in faith. I appreciate that you do not expect me to understand everything right away, but also that you do not allow me to plateau where I am. You are constantly encouraging me to take the next bite and grow.

How do you learn to distinguish good from evil?

REFUGE AND STRENGTH

God is our refuge and strength,
always ready to help in times of trouble.
So we will not fear when earthquakes come
and the mountains crumble into the sea.

PSALM 46:1-2 NLT

Since we have an eternal perspective and we know that God is our help in times of trouble, we can have confidence rather than fear when disaster strikes. When others are overcome with worry or doubt, we continue to focus on God and trust his hand will guide us.

Our strength and our courage come from God. Even if everything is crumbling down around us, we can find refuge in him because he is greater than the world. He is always prepared to offer his people comfort and hope in times of tragedy.

Grant me your understanding, Lord, and transform my worldly mindset. I do not worry about the future like those who are relying on themselves. I do not seek shelter behind temporary shields because you are my cover. I do not cower in the face of danger like those whose only defense is themselves. Lord, you alone are my refuge and my strength.

What is your initial reaction when catastrophe hits?

SPIRIT FILLED

Be filled with the Spirit, speaking to one another
with psalms, hymns, and songs from the Spirit.
Sing and make music from your heart to the Lord.
EPHESIANS 5:18-19 NIV

Paul cautioned Christians to not imitate the world or be controlled by its powers. This includes drunkenness, as mentioned just prior, since it could lead to depravity and ultimately ruin lives. Instead, he said we should be filled with the Spirit.

The Holy Spirit should be who controls us. This looks far different than the sloppy slurring effects of alcohol. When we are under the authority of the Holy Spirit, we are filled with joy, which leads to all sorts of praises and singing.

God, the joy you have put in my heart leads me to sing and shout your praises. I love to be in your presence, trusting in your power, filled with your Spirit, and glorifying your name.

What are the effects of being filled with the Spirit of God?

GLORY IN SUFFERING

We also glory in our sufferings, because we know that suffering produces perseverance; perseverance, character; and character, hope. And hope does not put us to shame, because God's love has been poured out into our hearts through the Holy Spirit, who has been given to us.

ROMANS 5:3-5 NIV

Accepting Christ as Lord and Savior does not mean an end to temporary pain and suffering this side of eternity. It does, however, give value to it. Rather than it simply being painful, it is now fruitful because it is working in us characteristics likened to Christ.

We also have a hope that will not disappoint: one day all our tears and sorrows will be wiped away and we will live in joy and freedom forever! That is not a promise the world can cling to in their time of trials.

Lord, thank you for taking my suffering and making something beautiful. You teach me how to persevere, you build my character, and you offer me hope. You are not a distant God who does not understand, for I know that you have similarly suffered all things, and therefore can fully relate to anything I encounter.

Although others may try to shame your faith, why does your hope vanquish their attempts?

GOOD MEDICINE

A joyful heart is good medicine,
but a crushed spirit dries up the bones.
PROVERBS 17:22 ESV

There is a clear connection between our emotional and physical wellbeing. The Lord created our bodies to operate as whole units, so to overlook a piece is to be negligent toward the entire thing. The Lord offers joy that is calming and healing. Although many aspects affect our overall heath, having a joyful spirit can offer a great deal of help to our overall wellness.

The Lord designed us to worship him. When we do, we experience his joy and peace because we are fulfilling our purpose. It will be better for our bodies than we could ever imagine. When our hearts are encouraged and we have something to put our hope in, it helps to strengthen and focus our entire bodies.

Thank you for your joy, dear Jesus! Thank you that, even if my circumstances are bad, I can still find joy in you amidst my sadness. Even if my body is aging and breaking down, you promise to give me a new body one day. You designed me so perfectly and I thank you for that.

How can joy help you physically?

LABOR IN THE LORD

My dear brothers and sisters, stand firm. Let nothing move you. Always give yourselves fully to the work of the Lord, because you know that your labor in the Lord is not in vain.

1 CORINTHIANS 15:58 NIV

At the conclusion of his letter, Paul offers his dear Corinthian brothers and sisters a final exhortation. First, they should stand firm, be steadfast, be faithful, and keep going. Continue in the teaching of the Lord and don't grow weary or be sidetracked. Second, Paul says to be immovable. Do not compromise values or conform to the culture out of pressure. Stand on the Word of God and do not be tossed around by a light form of Christianity.

Finally, Christians are to give themselves fully to their calling. Embrace the work the Lord calls us to and understand that it holds eternal importance. The fruit of our labor will not fade away because we serve an eternal Lord who remembers every act of faith.

Oh God, it is my desire to be committed, uncompromised, and joyfully obedient. Please take whatever faith I have to offer you and make something beautiful out of it.

What work has God given you to do? How can you give yourself fully to it?

LIVE TO SEE

I truly believe I will live to see the LORD's goodness.
PSALM 27:13 NCV

What the Lord says, he will accomplish. The promises in the Bible are not simple anecdotal whims or empty hopes. Our hope is rooted in Christ and is assured by his faithfulness. All the Lord's promises will be fulfilled and we will one day be in the presence of his goodness. In perfection, we will see the Lord face to face, and he will restore everything back to the way it was intended to be.

Recognizing this truth transforms our whole lives because we no longer live for fleeting gain. Every other pursuit is unworthy of the dedication of our lives because only what is of God will remain. We ought to use our lives now in preparation for eternity, rather than gather up worldly treasures which will only rust.

My God and Father, I live to see your goodness. Nothing else amounts to the anticipation of finally seeing you face to face. May my life be evidence of the truths I believe.

Do you truly believe you will see the Lord's goodness? What are you doing to prepare for that day?

TRUST

"Whoever can be trusted with very little can also be trusted with much, and whoever is dishonest with very little will also be dishonest with much."

LUKE 16:10 NIV

Those of us who have been given wealth ought to be faithful with it. If we have been given opportunities to exercise our faith, we should be diligent to do so. In all our relationships, it is important that we remain trustworthy. In whatever God has trusted us with, we have the option to be faithful or act dishonestly.

Sometimes it may feel like our circumstances would change if we had more; we could live honorably and not have a need to lie or cheat. The truth is, we never have a need to be dishonest because God will provide a way if we trust him. He is the same God whether we have a lot or a little.

Father, I know that honesty and dishonesty is a condition of my heart and shows whether I am relying on you or not. Rather than changing my condition, I ask that you change my heart. Please grow my faith and remind me that you are the same God in riches and in poverty.

How does dishonesty reveal a lack of trust in God?

UPHELD

*"Do not fear, for I am with you;
do not be dismayed, for I am your God.
I will strengthen you and help you;
I will uphold you with my righteous right hand."*

ISAIAH 41:10 NIV

The hand of God is available to anyone who will reach out and take it. He is always with us, protecting us and strengthening us. Whenever we feel afraid, we can be certain that God is nearby. Having faith that he loves us infinitely, we can cast aside our fear and have unmatched bravery.

It is God who upholds us by his righteousness. He defends us against our enemy and maintains our lives. He can pick us up when we feel disheartened and strengthen us through his power and might.

Uphold me with your righteous right hand, dear God. You never fail to rescue me from the enemy and strengthen me by your power and might. Remind me of your presence when I am afraid. My love for you is greater than my fear.

When you feel overwhelmed, how can you realize the unseen truths of God?

LORD OF PEACE

May the Lord of peace himself give you his peace at all times and in every situation. The Lord be with you all.

2 THESSALONIANS 3:16 NLT

Even though the church at Thessalonica harbored dissention and disrespectful members, Paul's prayer was for peace to reign over the entire congregation. In fact, he not only prayed that the Lord would send peace, but that the Lord of peace himself would be with them all as well.

No matter what situation we are faced with involving unbelievers or believers, the Lord offers his peace, which can lead us through any and all situations. There is no disagreement or circumstance that God's peace cannot prevail over. We are allotted that peace and it should be our sustenance through every difficulty.

Oh Lord of Peace, thank you for dwelling with me and filling me with your peace. There is no calamity that your peace cannot prevail over, and so I call on you today to bring order and calm to the chaos in my life.

How and when do you ask for and receive the peace of God?

FALL LIKE RAIN

Let my teaching fall on you like rain;
let my speech settle like dew.
Let my words fall like rain on tender grass,
like gentle showers on young plants.
DEUTERONOMY 32:2 NLT

Instead of compounding all his lessons on us and drowning us like a flood, the Lord patiently leads us to understanding, saturating us in his teaching like a gentle rain. He has so much grace for our ignorance and patience for our growth. He does not expect us to understand everything immediately but guides us through lessons and into maturity.

The Lord's words are life to those who are thirsty. They are like a drink of fresh water when we are weary. His revelations offer refreshment throughout the hard days, just like morning dew on the grass. It is by his words that we mature, and through his lessons that we grow stronger.

Like refreshing rain are your lessons upon me, dear Lord. I am feeble like the grass of the field. Daily, I require your grace and your nourishment. Without you I will simply fade away, but you fall on me like faithful rain and I soak in your teachings.

What has God taught you lately that refreshed you?

PASSION FOR LIFE

Let my passion for life be restored,
tasting joy in every breakthrough you bring to me.
Hold me close to you with a willing spirit
that obeys whatever you say.
PSALM 51:12 TPT

In John 15:10-11, Jesus makes it clear that the joy we experience directly correlates with our obedience to God. Here, David is asking God to restore his passion and his joy. He had broken God's commandments to not commit adultery or murder. Now, he wishes to stay close to God so he can walk in obedience, joy, and restoration.

Only God can completely restore what has been broken. He is willing to forgive the most atrocious sins and restore us to himself. We must, however, be willing to obey him, turn away from our wrongdoings, and stay close to him with a willing spirit.

Lord, disobedience only causes me turmoil and confusion. Because of your great love for me, you implemented commandments for me to follow. Often, I must come before you again for restoration and strength to willingly choose to do what is right. Please help me and hold me close.

What does it mean to have a willing spirit?

MAY

The grace of God
has appeared
that offers salvation
to all people.

TITUS 2:11 NIV

CLEAN HANDS

Those who do right will continue to do right,
and those whose hands are not dirty with sin will grow stronger.
JOB 17:9 NCV

Sin disguises itself as freedom, but it is a burden. Sin is a bondage that can pull down the strongest of us. The Lord is stronger, however, and he teaches us how to overcome sin. His Word is a guide and he fills us with power to endure. Although the will to do wrong feels overwhelming at times, the power to do what is right has been put in us; we simply need to learn how to use it.

When we are faced with an opportunity to sin, and we exercise the power to choose instead to do good, we grow stronger. Every sinful ploy that we cast down increases our competence and our confidence. As we learn to respond in the power of God, and habitually say no to sin, our strength increases and it becomes easier to do good.

How I desire my hands to be clean before you, God. Help me to choose to do what is right, so I can continue to live with integrity. Although you are quick to forgive, sin is a terrible trap from which it is difficult to break free. Please strengthen me to say no again and again.

Is there a sin that you feel powerless to prevent?

TRANSFORMED

Don't copy the behavior and customs of this world, but let God transform you into a new person by changing the way you think. Then you will learn to know God's will for you, which is good and pleasing and perfect.

ROMANS 12:2 NLT

The customs and systems of this world, which happen by default when our end goal is our own comfort and happiness, are not fitting for citizens of the eternal kingdom of God. We have been called to a higher standard and a different way of living.

It is our instinctual nature to chase those things which satisfy our fleshly longing, but we are to relinquish those pursuits for the sake of something far greater. Allowing God to lead and guide us will transform our desires and the way we think, and we will come to find out that his way is good, pleasing, and perfect.

In faith, I offer myself to you, dear God. I trust that your way is better than any way I would naturally choose. I surrender my own self-centered desires and ask that you reshape my mind to understand things from an eternal perspective.

What worldly pursuits keep you from pursuing God?

LISTEN TO ADVICE

The way of fools seems right to them,
but the wise listen to advice.
PROVERBS 12:15 NIV

Sometimes we become so convinced of our way that we shut down any offers of advice. In an effort to appear competent, we miss out on opportunities to increase our knowledge. None of us possess all understanding; we were designed to need other people.

Rather than insist on foolish behavior such as refusing to accept assistance, we should practice the wisdom of listening. If we humbly heed what others are trying to teach us, we could learn quite a bit and avoid many pitfalls. Wise people know that listening to advice is a far better option than protecting fragile self-images. Remain teachable. Be wise.

I pray for humility, Lord God, so that my pride does not threaten my ability to learn from others. Open my heart to hear what other people have to say and to consider their advice. Grant me the wisdom which comes from you.

Is it hard for you to accept advice? If so, why?

WORKING IN ME

God is working in you, giving you the desire and the power to do what pleases him.

PHILIPPIANS 2:13 NLT

It is the Spirit of God working in us that gives us the desire to do what pleases God as well as the strength and power to carry it out. Without God's help, we are left to the futility of our own flesh. When we are willing to be used by God, he readily takes over and uses us for his great work.

True faith comes with a willingness to serve God, which in turn gives an invitation to God to have his way in our lives. Incredible things can happen when a believer joyfully submits to God.

Come and have your way in my life, Heavenly Father. I want you to readjust my thinking so my vision is clear. Then, I wish to gladly participate in your work by following the calling you have put on me.

What desires has God placed in your heart? Do you honestly believe that he has also given you all the strength and power you need to carry out these desires?

BRAVE AND COURAGEOUS

Wait patiently for the LORD.
Be brave and courageous.
Yes, wait patiently for the LORD.
PSALM 27:14 NLT

Our position as Christians is to wait patiently. Our condition in which we are to wait is bravely and courageously. Our reward is the Lord. The task is daunting, but the prize is incredible. In this world we will encounter many forms of trouble. We are to face our problems with courage, for we know that the Lord is always near.

While confronting challenges, we are also called to wait patiently for the Lord. Although simple, this task is so difficult that David emphasized it a second time: patiently wait for God. As those who believe that Christ is coming back, we do not need to live a hurried, frantic way. Our eternal home is with the Lord, and the way we conduct ourselves ought to demonstrate our resolution to this end.

Lord, you make me brave. Because of the hope we have in you, we have courage enough to face anything this life throws at us. We wait patiently for your coming, knowing that you most assuredly will come. Thank you for our deliverance and for providing a way for us!

What does it look like in the life of a believer to be patiently waiting?

LOVE YOUR ENEMIES

*"I say to you, love your enemies.
Pray for those who hurt you."*
MATTHEW 5:44 NCV

It is not easy to love your enemies. Jesus did not command that we tolerate our enemies or peacefully avoid our enemies, but that we actually change our hearts to love them. The way we can do this is by actively praying for them. When we genuinely pray to God, our hearts begin to soften and change. We are invested in that for which we are praying.

We were Christ's enemies when we were outside of grace. He suffered the cross for our sake because he loves us. Now, in response to that unimaginable love, we are told to love others including our enemies.

Whether I am facing great persecution or menial offenses, my natural inclination is not to love my enemies or pray for them. Please change my heart, Lord Jesus, and make me more like you. I lift them up in prayer to you today, honestly asking for their forgiveness and change.

Who are your enemies? What is your prayer for them?

PERSUADING LEADERS

*Use patience and kindness when you want to persuade leaders
and watch them change their minds right in front of you.
For your gentle wisdom will quell the strongest resistance.*
PROVERBS 25:15 TPT

To enact an attack is to invite a retaliation. To enact change, however, demands a much more modest approach. When our intention is to change hearts, we should not be bothered about receiving the credit or promotion and praise. An unprecedented approach that does not shame or harm the other person can evoke an appreciation from them and perhaps even respect, rather than an onslaught that aims to protect their position and image.

This is especially true with leaders. Whether or not we agree with how our leaders are conducting themselves or handling matters, the Lord has put them in their role and he alone can see their hearts.

Lord, guide me in my confrontation so that I can avoid any unnecessary offense. Soften my heart so I can speak gently on behalf of you.

What is the best way for you to confront a leader in your life without inviting retaliation?

WISDOM FROM ABOVE

*The wisdom from above is first of all pure. It is also peace loving,
gentle at all times, and willing to yield to others. It is full of mercy
and the fruit of good deeds. It shows no favoritism and is always
sincere. And those who are peacemakers will plant seeds of peace
and reap a harvest of righteousness.*

JAMES 3:17-18 NLT

The philosophy of our physicality is me-centered. However,
the wisdom God offers is others-centered, and he promises to
take care of us.

We do not need to spend so much time worrying about
ourselves when we have the king of the universe promising to
watch over us. Take hold of this freedom, act wisely, and put
others first.

**Lord, make me wise. Help me put aside my contradictory
goals and look outward. Instead of always trying to meet
my own needs, teach me to consider others first and
look for opportunities to meet their needs. I want to be
peaceful, gentle, merciful, and sincere.**

*Living peacefully does not mean being ingenuine or
keeping silent. Are you willing to consider others and see
things from their perspective?*

LIKE JESUS

This is how love is made complete among us so that we will have confidence on the day of judgment: In this world we are like Jesus.
1 JOHN 4:17 NIV

True believers do not need to be afraid of the day of judgment because they know that their sins have been forgiven and they have been invited into God's family.

As family members, we should naturally seek to spend time with Jesus because we love him. In doing so, we become more like him. We learn from him. As we mature, we will resemble him more and more because he is working in us. When we show family traits and characteristics of Christ, we can be confident that we are truly in his family.

Jesus, the example your life set shook the entire world! The very idea that you are growing me to carry your image here on earth is mind-blowing. Thank you for being my kind and patient brother. Thank you for your leadership.

What Christ-like characteristics do you possess? What is he currently maturing in your life?

TRUST GOD

When I am afraid, I will trust you.
I praise God for his word.
I trust God, so I am not afraid.
What can human beings do to me?
PSALM 56:3-4 NCV

The true battles we fight are not against each other, but against the devil and his lies. Since God has already claimed victory over the devil, the victory is ours now. Yet, still the war continues. Those who have rejected Christ and have bought into the enemy's lies will consequentially reject us because Christ is in us.

Although our enemies may rise up against us, they have no power over us since they have no power over Christ. Even if they were to hurt our flesh, they cannot harm our souls. When we are afraid, we can trust that God is with us.

Malicious words are not truer than the words which you have spoken, Lord Jesus. I will choose to believe you rather than them. The wounds evil people inflict can never discredit the wounds you suffered on my behalf. I will choose to walk in your freedom rather than in fear. I trust you fully.

How does knowing the Word of God better and believing it in your heart help to cast out fear?

MANY WATERS

Many waters cannot quench love;
rivers cannot wash it away.
If one were to give all the wealth of his house for love,
it would be utterly scorned.

SONG OF SOLOMON 8:7 NIV

The constancy of true love in the face of seduction and adversity is one of the truest evidences of the Lord's presence here on earth. We were each created in God's image with love imprinted on our hearts. Those who reject God and pursue evil numb it or distort it. Those who deny God attribute it to another source. However, those of us who have placed our trust in God recognize his loving fingerprint on us and see its evidence in the form of true love.

Love is more powerful than the grave, as Christ demonstrated for us. It is stronger than temptation or self-interest. True love cannot be appeased or deterred by wealth or gain, for it only yearns for that which it loves. Anything short of the love of Christ will disappoint us.

The love you have shown me and the love you have placed in me is the greatest gift I could ever imagine, Lord God. I praise you for this fearless, prevailing love which compels me forward into your arms. Everything else in this world pales in comparison to your love.

What sort of waters and rivers try to drown out your love for Christ?

UNITED IN SPIRIT

Make every effort to keep yourselves united in the Spirit,
binding yourselves together with peace.

EPHESIANS 4:3 NLT

Paul knew how difficult it could be to live in community with others, and Jesus certainly did as well. It is still mandated because godly living is not nullified simply because it is hard. We have to make every effort to stay united as a body of believers, and that often means laying down our rights for the sake of a weaker sister or brother.

To live at peace, we must serve others, have grace on their weaknesses, bear their burdens, and share what we have. Peaceful living is not an easy assignment or one that will naturally happen without intentional action. We can collaboratively coexist, but the unity to which Paul directs us some translations have called the bond of peace. We are to live peacefully as if bound together.

God, I thank you for the way you have brought your family of believers together. Because you love me, I can love others. Please help me to overcome differences, conflicts, and self-seeking behavior so I can be unified with others for your glory.

What efforts can you take to live peacefully with those around you?

FRIENDSHIP

One who has unreliable friends soon comes to ruin,
but there is a friend who sticks closer than a brother.
PROVERBS 18:24 NIV

Friendships should not be overlooked or undervalued. Having someone to turn to, to help in our time of need, is worth more than storehouses of provisions. God has called us into community: to operate as a body and to care for one another's needs. If we walk alone, we have a better chance of falling or getting lost.

The friends we can rely on are worth far more than all the friendships who will flee when the path becomes steep. Friendships like these are likened to family and are worth investing in and praising God for.

Oh God, you are my king, but you have also shown that you want to be my friend. The very thought that you, the Almighty, wants to commune with me is incredible. Thank you for your friendship, God, and for always sticking with me despite it costing you so much.

Do you have a friend who you know will stick with you through anything? Are you that sort of friend?

RESTORATION

*The God of all grace, who called you to his eternal glory in Christ,
after you have suffered a little while, will himself restore you and
make you strong, firm and steadfast.*

1 PETER 5:10 NIV

God's grace goes much deeper than even his promise to
end all suffering: we will actually be restored from everything
that we have endured. We will no longer be broken or scarred
because he will build us up and make us strong.

Although we may feel weak or worn out, God will restore
to us everything that has been lost. All our hopes and desires
will be fulfilled and we will be made new. This world is passing
away, so we hold fast to our faith because God always keeps
his promises.

As if an end to all pain is not reward enough for those who
put their trust in you, you also promise to restore me to the
way you meant me to be, Father. You are strong, firm, and
steadfast, and you have made me in your likeness. Help me
to truly grasp what that means and what your intention is
for me.

*What do you imagine it will feel like when God removes
everything that hinders you and restores you fully to the
way he created you?*

DELIGHT IN THE LORD

Trust in the LORD and do good.
Then you will live safely in the land and prosper.
Take delight in the LORD,
and he will give you your heart's desires.

PSALM 37:3-4 NLT

Those whose trust is in the Lord are held securely in his hand. Although he may lead us through many dangers, there is no safer place to be. He is Lord of all, King of kings, and he promises to protect us. His Word teaches us how we ought to live in order to prosper. When we choose to do good, the outcomes will obviously be better for us and we will thrive.

If our delight is in the Lord, then our desire is for him. If our desire is for the Lord, then he will not disappoint but will fill our desire. When we clearly realize how satisfying, exciting, and fulfilling a life in Christ is, then all other desires seem to fade. Living for him is the most delightful and desirable life imaginable.

I trust in you, oh Lord, and I delight fully in you. Nothing else satisfies like you do, for everything else leaves me thirsty in the end. You fill me up continually, and you reveal to me the true desires of my heart.

Why does it seem like evil people prosper? What does it mean to you to prosper in God's kingdom?

LOVE ONE ANOTHER

"A new commandment I give to you, that you love one another: just as I have loved you, you also are to love one another."

JOHN 13:34 ESV

Christ came not only to free us from death, but also to save us from our destructive ways. He demonstrated for us the way to live and then asked that we follow his example. He taught us the perfect paradoxes between his kingdom and our selfish natures and invited us to live for others rather than ourselves. He loved us with an unrelenting love and told us to love others the same way.

To love one another is the trademark of the Christian life. We cannot claim to have known the love of Christ or to have heard his teachings if we fail to love each other because that is the basis of the Bible. God is love, and his followers will walk as he does.

God, help me not draw lines between who I will love and who I won't. Give me love for sinners, for people who offend me, and for those who reject me.

Do you think the Scriptures would repeat the importance of loving people if it were easy? Who do you find difficult to love?

NEVER FORSAKEN

"I will bring the blind by a way they did not know;
I will lead them in paths they have not known.
I will make darkness light before them, and crooked places straight.
These things I will do for them, and not forsake them."

ISAIAH 42:16 NKJV

Our limited understanding and unknown future render us blind. The Lord will not forsake us to navigate our own way through the dark. He offers to guide us and lead us down paths we do not know. He is our shining light that illuminates our view and overcomes the darkness. We will never get lost while submitting to his leadership.

Sometimes we can fool ourselves into thinking we know what is going on, and we fall back on self-reliance. This is not a sure foundation, as we will quickly realize.

Father, wherever there is confusion, you are present with answers. Crooked paths you make straight and darkness you make light. Your Word guides me like the most reliable map. Thank you for never forsaking me and for always remaining nearby.

Who opens your eyes to true understanding?

PROMISES FULFILLED

All of God's promises have been fulfilled in Christ with a resounding "Yes!" And through Christ, our "Amen" (which means "Yes") ascends to God for his glory.

2 CORINTHIANS 1:20 NLT

Christ was the fulfillment of all that God had promised throughout the Old Testament. He provided various pictures throughout history to prove the Lordship of Jesus, so that when he came, we would recognize him and realize that God always does what he says. He is completely trustworthy.

As children of God, we ought to resemble our Father. Rather than constantly changing our minds as our desires lead us, we should be resolute and dependable. We will not always have the answers, and we may at times learn of a better way, but when we say yes or no, we should be prepared to follow through. When we make a promise, we should be prepared to fulfill that promise.

I have full confidence in you, God because you always keep your word. Regardless of my disobedience toward you, the promises you made you are resolved to keep. Please teach me to stay committed to my word even when the excitement is gone. I want to be like you.

Is there a promise you have made that is hard to keep? What helps you stay true to it?

ALIVE AND ACTIVE

The word of God is alive and active. Sharper than any double-edged sword, it penetrates even to dividing soul and spirit, joints and marrow; it judges the thoughts and attitudes of the heart.
HEBREWS 4:12 NIV

The Word of God is not simply a historic document that we are intended to arbitrarily read and study for the sake of obedience only. God's words are active and living. They provide a guideline for our lives and the answers to so many questions.

To simply search the Bible for a moment and a quick answer may not reveal much, but when we truly know it, live by it, and take it to heart, our attitude changes and answers are revealed. Only God's Word has the ability to discern all things, see deep into our souls, and distinguish righteousness from unrighteousness.

Lord, thank you for your Word. I praise you for your direction in my life and for being a gracious, loving, and protective Father. Without your Word to guide me, I would be like a lost sheep. May I never take it for granted, Lord, but live by its teachings daily and in all things.

What does the analogy of the sharp sword reveal about the Word of God?

MY ROCK

Truly he is my rock and my salvation;
he is my fortress, I will never be shaken.

PSALM 62:2 NIV

Any promise of security outside of God is like shifting sand. If we are finding safety in success, wealth, popularity, or our own abilities, the sands could shift at any moment and it will all cave in.

God alone is the rock on which we can build with a guarantee of protection. He is like a strong fortress where we can run in times of trouble. Our enemies cannot pursue us past the reach of God. Although we may be attacked, we cannot be shaken if we are resting in the Lord and building upon the rock of our salvation.

Lord, you are my firm foundation. You are the immovable rock I choose to fasten my faith to. Thank you for your unwavering love and your impenetrable protection. Hold me, Lord, so I will not be shaken when I am attacked. You are the fortress I run to.

How does building a house on rock compare to building a house on sand?

FORGIVENESS

Bear with each other, and forgive each other. If someone does wrong to you, forgive that person because the Lord forgave you.
COLOSSIANS 3:13 NCV

As family members, we should be quick to forgive and to help each other succeed. If we truly understand what Christ did for us and what he saved us from, then forgiveness should be our natural response. Everything we have is because of the grace of God poured on us, so we are to show each other the same grace.

This verse is not instructing us to be apathetic toward sin or stay silent in the face of injustice but to forgive the wrongs done to us and help others to bear the burdens of their weaknesses. This way, growth can occur and the grace we have been shown is made evident by the way we show grace to others.

Oh God, I thank you for your forgiveness and your grace. I was lost to sin without your intervention. Since you have restored my life and hope, I dare not withhold forgiveness from others. Sometimes it is difficult to see past my offense, so I ask for your help to heal my heart and love my offender the way you do.

Is there anyone you need to forgive today?

NO LONGER SLAVES

We know that our old life died with Christ on the cross so that our sinful selves would have no power over us and we would not be slaves to sin.

ROMANS 6:6 NCV

When Christ died for us on the cross, he took the weight of sin and death with him. Metaphorically, when we accept Jesus as our Lord and Savior, our old sin natures die and no longer hold any claim to our lives.

Although we may still battle the same temptations or shortcomings as we did before, we are no longer their slaves. Jesus has the power over our lives, and he is our Master. We can rejoice because we are now ruled by love and grace, rather than sin and death.

With my whole life I will love you, Lord Jesus. I praise you because you have released my bonds and freed me from sin's snares. My freedom offers me so many opportunities to serve you and others on your behalf, and I want to make the most of it. Teach me how, dear Jesus.

Do you still feel like your old sin holds some sort of power over you? Have you fully realized the cleansing and renewing power of Jesus Christ?

ENCOURAGEMENT

Worry weighs a person down;
an encouraging word cheers a person up.
PROVERBS 12:25 NLT

When worry overtakes us, being reminded of the truth can offer great reprieve. A true friend provides encouragement and cheer, helping the worried to lift their burdens. Worry is like a weight that pulls us down. It imagines the possible negative outcomes and fixates on failures. Worry forgets the Lord's faithfulness and forgoes his help.

By simply offering an encouraging word, we have the power to reassure others and restore their hope. It may not seem like words carry much weight, but they have the power to break someone down or build them up. We should strive to be responsible and loving in the way we use our words.

Your words inspire me and fill me with hope, Father. I find so much encouragement in the words of your Scriptures. Please give me wisdom to be an encouragement to others as well. Help me to overcome worry with faith and to support others as they strive to do the same.

How do you know what to say to someone in their worry? What is an example of an encouraging word?

NEARNESS

Let your gentleness be evident to all. The Lord is near.

PHILIPPIANS 4:5 NIV

The Lord is near and is returning soon. Sometimes it may not seem like soon enough, but we can make the most of our time until then by obeying his laws and living the way he showed us to. We are to be gentle. Gentleness, from the Greek word epieikes, has also been translated as reasonableness. It gives the idea of handling situations carefully and with wisdom.

Paul had just intervened in a public argument between two women of the Philippian church. Rather than being unreasonable and allowing their disagreement to cause a division, Paul identified them both as fellow laborers in the work of the Lord and pleaded with them to be unified. He asked other believers to support them, told them to rejoice, and instructed that they allow their gentleness to be on display. When we argue, it should be self-controlled and in the hope of procuring peace.

God, lead me into unity and gentleness with others. I pray against division and ask that you fill me with your wisdom.

How should knowing that the Lord is nearby influence your perspective and behavior?

HOPE IN THE LORD

All you who put your hope in the LORD
be strong and brave.
PSALM 31:24 NCV

When troubling circumstances befall us, we cannot give in to despondency. Our hope must be in the Lord in the good times as well as the bad. Although scenarios change, God's faithfulness remains constant. Knowing that he loves us and will never leave us should empower us with the strength and courage to endure.

Christians are not exempt from the world's difficulties. In fact, we may encounter more of them since we follow the system of a different kingdom. Unlike those who rely on themselves, we have guaranteed help from the Almighty who strengthens us and makes us brave.

I hope in you, Lord, in every type of trial. Even in my weakness, my hope in you makes me strong. I know the outcome of my faith, and the consequences for not relying on you are grim. Teach me to walk in the confidence I feel, to take heart, and to be bold.

How can you be strong and brave when you feel weak and afraid?

DIVISION

*Jesus knew their thoughts and said to them, "Every kingdom
divided against itself will be ruined, and every city or household
divided against itself will not stand."*
MATTHEW 12:25 NIV

It is important that we pursue peace with our sisters and
brothers when at all possible. If we are constantly bickering
and drawing lines, then we look just like the rest of the world.
Who would be able to recognize Christ in us? God has knit us
together as family members, so we must not rend his work apart.

Divisions threaten to undo our witness. How can we
operate as a body if we are at war? There is a time for
discussing matters to grow and to learn, and there is a time to
lay matters aside for the sake of our work and unity.

**Jesus, the people looked for any excuse to discredit you.
When you healed the man who was demon possessed, they
claimed it must have been because you were aligned with
demons. If people falsely accuse me, may it not demoralize
me. Give me insight, Lord, to continue to insist on doing
good and on proclaiming my allegiance to you.**

Who is affected when the body of Christ is divided?

EVERLASTING LOVE

"I have loved you with an everlasting love;
I have drawn you with unfailing kindness."

JEREMIAH 31:3 NIV

The Israelites often turned away from God in favor of other idols or of themselves. Then, when they faced persecution, they would run back to the Lord. Over and over, he received them back. He does not turn aside a contrite heart. True repentance should not present only when help is needed, but the Lord understood the weakness of the Israelites and continued to welcome them home, showing them unfailing kindness.

Even when our faith is weak, the Lord will accept us if we ask. He helps us to mature in faith and gives us ample amounts of grace. His love is everlasting and his compassion is certain.

I praise you for your everlasting love. You are great and your mercy is undeniable. Thank you for forgiving my sins again and again, for calling me back to yourself, and for treating me as a true heir of your kingdom. I love you.

When you try to forge your own way, do you sense the Lord drawing you back to himself?

GREAT GAIN

Godliness with contentment is great gain, for we brought nothing into the world, and we cannot take anything out of the world. But if we have food and clothing, with these we will be content.

1 TIMOTHY 6:6-8 ESV

Paul told Timothy that some of the identifying attributes of false teachers were their greed and desire for wealth. To put our priorities into perspective, Paul reminded us that we came into this world with nothing and that is just how we will exit it.

Everything we have been given is a gift, and we should be grateful regardless of whether we have been allotted great wealth or just enough. Greed is not fitting of a child of God. We can have true contentment because our hope is in Christ Jesus.

In you, I find my resting place, dearest Father. You have filled my heart with joy and contentment, and you have supplied me with everything we need. You take great care of the birds and the flowers, and I know you love me so much more intimately. Thank you for everything you have blessed me with today.

When you see others with something you desire, does it cause you to doubt God's love or provision?

BOOK OF THE LAW

Keep this Book of the Law always on your lips; meditate on it day and night, so that you may be careful to do everything written in it. Then you will be prosperous and successful.

JOSHUA 1:8 NIV

The Bible is not an obligatory book of rules and laws, it is our path to freedom. God knows what we need and never fails to provide for us. One of the ways he has done this is by giving us his living Word. The Scriptures are full of instructions on how we can live the life we were meant to, thus experiencing fullness of joy in finding our true potential.

Life apart from God is futile. It can appear exciting, but it is empty and void of purpose. True success and prosperity in a way that has eternal worth can be attained by holding to the lessons found in the Bible.

Teach me your ways, oh Lord, and open my mind to understand your teachings. Within your Word there is life and prosperity. I want to ponder it daily, and have its truths ever on my lips.

What sort of instructions does the Bible give for daily life?

WAIT QUIETLY

Let all that I am wait quietly before God,
for my hope is in him.
PSALM 62:5 NLT

Rather than amassing wealth in an attempt to gain security, we are to hope in the Lord. Relationships will not protect us when the end of all things comes. There is no ability that we possess that can save us from the conniving of the devil. Only those whose hope is rooted in God will be preserved.

We wait patiently for God because his saving grace is assured. We do not cry out as those who have no hope because the truth has been given to us. Although we are afflicted, this is not the end. We are not frantic; we are confident and calm. Everything in us can rest in the promises of God as we quietly wait for his perfect timing.

I am resigned to you, God, for you alone hold my fate in your hands. I am at peace because you have proven yourself to be faithful and sure. My spirit is not restless; it is calm and content. Whenever I come to you in prayer, please renew my hope and quiet any restlessness or worry that may have found a place within me. My hope is in you alone.

When anxiety creeps in, how do you quiet your heart again?

DESTRUCTION

If you bite and devour each other,
watch out or you will be destroyed by each other.
GALATIANS 5:15 NIV

Why would we waste the incredible freedom we have been given on living the way the world lives? To live according to our own betterment alone is empty, isolating, and a horrible misuse of the grace we have been shown. If every believer only lived for themselves, there would be a whole body of contradictory agendas which would cause conflict and collisions at every turn.

Aware that this kind of living would ultimately destroy us, Jesus laid out a better plan: he would fight for us, and we should fight for each other.

Lord, you are worthy of my surrender. Rather than esteeming myself and vying for the best seat, please humble me and fill me with love for others. Show me who I can serve today and how I can put their needs before my own. I know that you are taking care of me, so I can take care of others.

Who can you step aside for today?

JUNE

If he chose them by grace,
it is not for the things they have
done. If they could be made
God's people by what they did,
God's gift of grace would
not really be a gift.

ROMANS 11:6 NCV

GOD IS WITH YOU

"Be strong and courageous, and do the work. Don't be afraid or discouraged, for the LORD God, my God, is with you. He will not fail you or forsake you. He will see to it that all the work related to the Temple of the LORD is finished."

1 CHRONICLES 28:20 NLT

When God commissions us to do something, he always gives us what we need to succeed. Even if the odds seem stacked against us, there is much going on that we cannot see. In certain times, we can only trust the Lord's goodness to see us through.

In any task, work diligently as unto the Lord, for it is he who we serve. He equips us with strength and courage, helps us to stand resolute in the face of fear, and will never leave our side. What we start, he will help us finish. He does not forsake us to fight alone. Take hold of his power and trust that God is with us.

You are the same God today as you were in the time of King David. You are mightier than the mountains I see before me. If there are obstacles standing in the way of me and what you have called me to, please give me the faith to know that I will overcome them by your strength.

Has God ever called you to something that you felt was too much for you to handle?

GIFTS FROM GOD

If your gift is serving, then serve. If it is teaching, then teach. Is it encouraging others? Then encourage them. Is it giving to others? Then give freely. Is it being a leader? Then work hard at it. Is it showing mercy? Then do it cheerfully.

ROMANS 12:7-8 NIRV

We have each been given different gifts, but the same command: use them. Without comparing or complaining, we should embrace the unique way God has created us by diligently using our gifts to serve others, thus bringing glory to God.

Our talents are not intended to simply serve our own whims, for we are called to a greater purpose than that. Furthermore, we are not to covet each other's gifts and skills. God has commissioned each of us and equipped us differently. Rather than looking around at others, let us look to our Creator as he reveals more about us than we ever knew.

I have been carefully crafted to reflect a piece of you, Almighty God. Thank you for the honor of bearing your image. Help me also display your greatness by using my gifts in service to you and others.

What are your God-given gifts?

GRACIOUSNESS

One who is gracious to a poor man lends to the Lord,
and He will repay him for his good deed.

PROVERBS 19:17 NASB

When we give to those who cannot repay us, it is as if we are giving straight to God. The way we demonstrate our love for the Lord is by loving each other. When we are gracious to others, God will be gracious to us. When we forgive others, God will forgive us. When we give to others without an expectation for compensation, the Lord will certainly remember and repay us for our faithfulness.

The Lord is tremendously generous; we cannot outgive him. He sees every good deed and will not forget the generosity and grace we show to others. It is as if we are loving him directly.

My love for you, God, spurs me on to love others. Rather than looking for what I can get, change my heart to consider what I can give. Reveal needs to me, Lord, that you are leading me to address. Bring me people to love and people to support who may never pay me back.

Who can you give to, knowing they cannot return the favor?

PRAYERS AND PETITIONS

*Do not be anxious about anything, but in every situation, by prayer
and petition, with thanksgiving, present your requests to God. And
the peace of God, which transcends all understanding, will guard
your hearts and your minds in Christ Jesus.*

PHILIPPIANS 4:6-7 NIV

In a world full of worries and concerns, we can be free
from anxiety. Although threats are constantly looming and the
plight of the earth continues to darken, we have peace.

As Christians, we are not spared from trouble, but we do
serve an omnipotent God who hears and answers us. He is a
peaceful God who promises to guard us. With thankfulness,
we should turn to prayer rather than panic when difficult times
come upon us.

**When everyone around me is stressed and anxious, I will
choose to bring my fears and uncertainties to you, Lord.
I will lay them at your feet and choose to focus on you. I
thank you for your goodness and your peace. Please, strip
away my anxiety and guard my heart and mind.**

*Are you trying to control something that God has invited
you to trust him with? Can you bring it before him in prayer
and leave it with him?*

MEEKNESS

The meek shall inherit the land
and delight themselves in abundant peace.
PSALM 37:11 ESV

It is through meekness that we learn to listen to our Father's voice. We carefully consider his words and act upon them. To be meek is to be submissive to the Father. Meek people are not rebellious or loud. They possess self-control and trust. Their character cannot be shaken because it is in agreement with God's will.

The Lord promises the world to those who walk in meekness. They will not be disappointed for obeying his directions. In fact, they will be rewarded with abundant peace. He is their delight, and he also delights in them.

Father, lead me in your better way. Quiet my heart and mind so I learn to recognize your voice in the midst of the chaos. I do not want to resemble the world, with its self-gratification and its provocative ploys. It teaches me to live for my own happiness, but I want to live for you. In turn, you grant me joy and peace, and I praise you for that.

How did Jesus demonstrate meekness?

ONE MASTER

"No one can serve two masters. Either you will hate the one and love the other, or you will be devoted to the one and despise the other. You cannot serve both God and money."

MATTHEW 6:24 NIV

The mentality of the world contradicts the law of God. The former teaches us to seek our own happiness, where the latter commands that we look out for the welfare of others. Money and material wealth can be used at tools for great purposes, but if these earthly riches captivate us and steal our devotion, God will not be pleased. He does not wish to take second seat to anything, and we cannot serve him if we are serving ourselves.

The Lord desires to be our one and only master. He rules in love and all his ways are just. He has guaranteed us eternal life, peace, joy, and family. His love for us is everlasting and unparalleled. We should not throw this all to the side in pursuit of any lesser master.

You are my master, dearest Lord, and I choose to worship you alone. When other trinkets catch my eye, remind me of who I serve. Your glory is matchless and I have all that I could ever hope for or imagine in you.

What is the difference between serving money and having money?

NOT DISAPPOINTED

Don't envy sinners, but always continue to fear the Lord.
You will be rewarded for this; your hope will not be disappointed.
PROVERBS 23:17-18 NLT

The glory of sin is short lived and costly. The glory of the Lord is everlasting and generous. He has rewards aplenty for those who choose to trust him; relying on his goodness rather than their own gain.

The ends do not justify the means where the Lord is concerned, for he will always provide a way for us to walk in righteousness and still achieve his ends. God did not promise that his path would be easy or without pain. He did, however, assure us that we would not be disappointed.

Following you is its own reward, God, and still you lavishly reward me with gifts beyond imagination. Your way is truly the best way. Perhaps, at times, it is the more arduous and less attractive, but I know that if I continue to follow you, it will all be more than worth it.

How does fearing the Lord resolve you to not follow the way of sinners?

PIONEER AND PROTECTOR

Looking to Jesus the pioneer and perfecter of our faith, who for the sake of the joy that was set before him endured the cross, disregarding its shame, and has taken his seat at the right hand of the throne of God.

HEBREWS 12:2 NRSV

After introducing so many heroes of the faith in Hebrews 11, the writer encourages Christians to draw confidence from their testimonies and similarly throw off anything which would hinder them from running the spiritual race that has been set before them.

The way we can endure all hardship and persevere is by keeping our eyes locked on Jesus. There are limitless distractions in this life, but Christ stands as an unadulterated paradox to them all. His faith was focused and flawless. Now he has given us that same faith and an unmatched example to follow.

Jesus, may you be highly exalted. Amid the anguish of your sacrifice, it actually brought you joy because of your great love for me. Now, as you rightfully sit as King, I ask that you strengthen me to run the race you have given me to run.

What is the prize or the joy you are running for?

WORLDLY DESIRES

All that is in the world—the desires of the flesh and the desires of the eyes and pride in possessions—is not from the Father but is from the world.

1 John 2:16 esv

What John is addressing here is not our natural desires for basic needs, or our attraction to beautiful things. He is refuting lust and excessive indulgence. The danger he is combatting is when we value anything higher than God Almighty.

By following our flesh, we are not submitting to God's leadership. When we take pride in our possessions or positions, we are not honoring him first or giving him the well-earned glory. We should be proud to be his children.

The greatest riches, most satisfying indulgences, and the most remarkable of sights all pale in comparison to your wonder and glory, Lord God. You are my truest desire, and I will boast in you alone and what you have accomplished in me.

What is the difference between taking pleasure in what God has created, and lusting for more and more?

ROCK AND REFUGE

Be my rock of refuge, to which I can always go;
give the command to save me, for you are my rock and my fortress.
Deliver me, my God, from the hand of the wicked,
from the grasp of those who are evil and cruel.
For you have been my hope, Sovereign Lord,
my confidence since my youth.

PSALM 71:3-5 NIV

The Lord is permanently close by, offering refuge and rest in any circumstance. We can always go to him for safety and reassurance. He commands his angels to keep watch over us, rescuing us from the attacks of our enemies.

God is the steadfast rock on which our hope is found. Since God has shown from the beginning of time that he is immovable, we can be confident that our hope will not be disappointed.

You truly are the Sovereign Lord, the same today as you have always been. You are a mighty fortress, offering refuge for your weary followers. You are the rock I stand confidently on. You are my deliverance and hope forever.

What sort of attacks have you been facing that you need a place of refuge from?

NO EVIL

Render true judgments, show kindness and mercy to one another,
do not oppress the widow, the fatherless, the sojourner, or the poor,
and let none of you devise evil against another in your heart.
ZECHARIAH 7:8-10 ESV

Children of God should not be meddling in evil affairs. Since we know where our provisions come from, there is no reason we should cheat anyone or submit inaccurate accounts. Kindness and mercy should be our way, and we should devise plans to do good.

The Lord has a tender spot in his heart for the helpless and the disadvantaged. This may be someone who has lost their spouse and is reliant on one income. It could be someone who does not have the support of parents. It is perhaps the foreigners who are immersed in a culture that is not their own. Most certainly, it includes the poor. These are the people we are to run to show kindness and mercy to.

God, I want to walk in a way that is true, and kind, and merciful toward everyone, especially those who are hurting and need it most. People are never a means to my own ends; they are each dearly beloved by you.

Do you know someone who is disadvantaged and could use your help?

GOD'S HANDIWORK

We are God's handiwork, created in Christ Jesus to do good works,
which God prepared in advance for us to do.

EPHESIANS 2:10 NIV

Salvation is not given to us because of our good works, but by it we can accomplish good works. God calls us his handiwork or workmanship or artwork. He designed us carefully and intentionally with a plan in mind for each of us. Good works are the result of salvation, not the other way around.

God has laid out a plan and a purpose for each of us. There is no need to try and copy someone else's calling because God has something more fitting in mind. We only need to trust him and follow his leading, and everything will be revealed in its timing.

Lord, lead me and teach me to accomplish the good works you have specifically designed me to do. My desire is to be your hands and feet on the earth.

Do you recognize that you are God's artwork, masterfully crafted for the purpose of bringing him praise? How were you uniquely created?

WALK WITH THE WISE

Whoever walks with the wise becomes wise,
but the companion of fools suffers harm.
PROVERBS 13:20 NRSV

Habits and behaviors are learned. We are far more susceptible to influence than we would like to imagine, and the more we associate with foolishness, the sooner we will resemble fools.

This does not mean we ought to reject those who do wrong, since Jesus himself sat with sinners and sought out the lost. But we should surround ourselves with those who are also walking wisely because we are bound to become more like them. Influence is powerful, and so we must purposefully decide what we will allow to influence us.

I love to be in your presence, Father, for you bring sense to the confusion around me. You impart your wisdom to those who seek you, and you also encourage me to seek other wise people. Please bring those people into my life and give me humility to learn from them. Walk with me today, God.

Do you associate with wise people in an effort to learn from them?

BROTHERLY LOVE

*Have unity of mind, sympathy, brotherly love,
a tender heart, and a humble mind.*

1 PETER 3:8 ESV

Peter addressed certain groups, such as husbands and wives, slaves and masters, and so on. At this point, however, he addresses everyone. These are not virtues for select people or certain situations; this is the calling of every person who follows Christ.

God intends his followers to be a family. As a community of like-minded people, we can encourage each other and walk together, thus having greater impact and fortitude. We are to be sympathetic with each other. Our hearts should not grow hardened, but we are to remain tender and show sympathy. In line with God's intention to forge a family, brotherly love and humility are imperative.

Lord, help me to lay down myself for the sake of others. I want to humbly pursue what is collectively good, rather than striving for my own advancement. Help me to be one who encourages familial love and a unified mind with other believers.

Why does God want you to work in community rather than on your own?

PLEASED WITH ME

I know that you are pleased with me,
for my enemy does not triumph over me.
Because of my integrity you uphold me
and set me in your presence forever.
PSALM 41:11-12 NIV

The Lord upholds his people. Those who place their trust in him, he will faithfully protect. The devil cannot snatch us from the hand of God. He is holding us, finding pleasure in us, since all the devil's attacks against us have proven unsuccessful.

Because of God's grace, we are forgiven of all our sins. This grace touches our hearts and compels us to have integrity. By our integrity, the Lord recognizes a changed and renewed heart, and he brings us into his presence. Our salvation is by God's grace alone, and we cannot remain unchanged upon receiving it.

Please find pleasure in me, Father. Thank you for thwarting all my enemy's plots against me, and for setting me in your presence. In order to be in your presence, I must be found guiltless, and because of your grace, I am.

How do you know that God is pleased with you?

GRIEF AND JOY

"You too have grief now; but I will see you again, and your heart will rejoice, and no one will take your joy away from you."

JOHN 16:22 NASB

Jesus told his disciples of the sorrow they were about to bear at his crucifixion. Those around them would rejoice and they would mourn. They were not to be surprised or dismayed by this because they would surely see Jesus again.

Although death and sin rob from us now and inflict us with grief, they cannot withhold our joy. A day is coming when all will be restored, when the Lord will enact his final judgement and Jesus Christ will return for us. Since we have an eternal, Biblical mindset, there are instances when we grieve and the world around us celebrates. What is right and what is wrong seem to be mixed up. This will not last. One day, Jesus will turn the tables and our sorrow will be transformed into joy that nothing can destroy.

Jesus, you turn my mourning into dancing and my grief into joy. The devil tries to steal my joy, and although he can impose many wounds on me now, I remember the end you have planned for those who follow you.

What do you rejoice over that the world scoffs at? What grieves you that the world promotes?

ETERNAL LORD

"Even from eternity I am He,
and there is none who can deliver out of My hand;
I act and who can reverse it?"
Isaiah 43:13 NASB

We are finite beings, but the Lord Almighty is infinite. Our presence here is fixed, but he is eternal. We were created by him, the author of all that we know. What he has decided to do, none can dismantle. Whom he decides to save, none can sway.

The Lord extends his hand and delivers us from our adversary, and all the enemy's schemes cannot crush his saving power. He is from eternity, possessing all forms of love and wisdom. His plan is good and we are a part of it.

Before time began, you were there. You exist apart from me, but I do not exist apart from you. For your glory, you decided to create me, and it is my greatest pleasure to love you and worship you in return. Your intricate plan for the world includes my deliverance, and what you have put into motion nobody can stop. I praise you, for you are the eternal Lord.

Who does the Lord deliver?

RENEWED

*We do not lose heart. Though outwardly we are wasting away,
yet inwardly we are being renewed day by day. For our light and
momentary troubles are achieving for us an eternal glory that far
outweighs them all. So we fix our eyes not on what is seen,
but on what is unseen, since what is seen is temporary,
but what is unseen is eternal.*

2 CORINTHIANS 4:16-18 NIV

It is easy to lose sight of what matters in lieu of what is daily in front of our faces. One of the devil's evil ploys is simply to keep us distracted: sidetracked from what really matters and what we are called to do.

In order to overcome, we must keep our eyes fixed on Jesus. Since he is unseen, that means remaining focused on what he has told us and shown us. In all things, we must not lose heart.

Although life may break me down, you are actually working through my hardships to renew my mind and refocus my heart. I do not look at troubles the same way the world does because I submit to your higher form of thinking. The world and its comforts are temporary, but your unseen promises are eternal.

Why do troubles help to achieve glory?

ASSEMBLING TOGETHER

Let us consider how to stimulate one another to love and good deeds, not forsaking our own assembling together, as is the habit of some, but encouraging one another; and all the more as you see the day drawing near.

HEBREWS 10:24-25 NASB

All throughout Scripture, God's intention for us to live as a community of believers is revealed. He created us to need each other so we could learn how to put others first and lay ourselves down. Here, we are reminded to encourage others toward love and good works.

We are not to neglect other Christians. In fact, we have a biblical responsibility to fellowship with others so that we can continue to learn and grow through relationships, and so we can help bear their burdens and encourage them.

Oh God, I love my relationships, but they are also sometimes the most difficult element of life. Rather than moving on when they become strained or require maintenance, teach me how to fight for love and unity in my family of faith.

When it becomes difficult to be around someone, how do you respond to the situation? Do you humble yourself and attempt to amend the relationship?

UNDIVIDED

Teach me your way, Lord,
that I may rely on your faithfulness;
give me an undivided heart,
that I may fear your name.
PSALM 86:11 NIV

The fear of the Lord leads to proper reverence for who he is. His ways are far superior to ours, and it benefits us greatly when we follow his ways rather than our own. Instead of depending on ourselves, we rely on the tried and true faithfulness of God.

Our hearts must be undivided because otherwise we will be torn in different directions. We cannot serve two masters, so we must either choose ourselves or God. Since he has proven to be far more faithful than we are, the vastly better decision is to give our allegiance to him.

Give me an undivided heart, Lord, and fill me with reverent fear. May my own selfish desires be cast aside as I learn to rely on you. Your faithfulness is unbroken, yet I have stumbled many times. Please help me to never seek myself over you, but to choose you every time with a heart that is resolved to do your will.

What other interests threaten to divide your heart?

IN JESUS' NAME

Whatever you do, whether in word or deed, do it all in the name of the Lord Jesus, giving thanks to God the Father through him.

COLOSSIANS: 3:17 NIV

Throughout his letters, Paul penned many specific dos and don'ts for Christians to adhere to. There would be no way for him—or anyone—to address every situation, so he summarizes that, whatever we do, it should be for the sake of the Lord Jesus.

Every action we take and every word we speak should be aligned with the life we claim to live in Christ.

Father God, as you continue to disciple me, my faith matures and I become more in tune with your heart and how you want me to conduct myself. The deeper my relationship with you grows, the less I need an outlined checklist of proper behavior because whatever I do is for you and in your name. Thank you for being my guide.

Do you habitually end your prayers by saying "in Jesus' name"? Have you considered what you are implying by this?

UNSEEN

If we hope for what we do not see,
we wait for it with patience.
ROMANS 8:25 ESV

Although we cannot see the future glory that God has promised us, we hope for it in full confidence because we know that God always keeps his word. Since the beginning of time, the Lord has demonstrated and documented for us a perfect track record of his faithfulness. He is not asking us to take a leap of faith but to follow his tried and true leadership.

As Christians, walking through this life means that we know the best is not now. One day, everything will be fulfilled, corrected, and restored. We do not live for the moment, but with our eternal inheritance at heart. It is our motivation and our reason behind the decisions we make. We must wait patiently. When those around us are living for this world and for the moment, we must put our hope in the Lord.

You know the best way and the best timing for everything, Lord. I will continue to live for you and put my hope in you alone because this world is passing away and it is not worthy of my devotion. Even though I cannot see you, you have made sure I can witness the worthwhileness of following you.

What are you hoping for?

SUCCESS

*Those who get wisdom do themselves a favor,
and those who love learning will succeed.*
PROVERBS 19:8 NCV

Wisdom is so worthwhile, and it will be a great favor to those who receive it. Job amounted the worth of wisdom to greater than that of the most precious stones. He pointed out that men will move mountains and tear apart the earth in their quest to uncover jewels, yet wisdom is of much greater value and so readily attainable. It comes from a proper fear of the Lord.

In order to learn, we must be humble and teachable. If we want to succeed, we have to be willing to receive correction from others. Those who love learning, and truly seek to grow and mature, will certainly find success.

I long for your wisdom, Lord, so I might know your will and walk in your ways. I love to learn from your Word, and I take your lessons to heart. Help me to succeed in all that I do. I give you the glory forever, dear Lord.

Do you consider yourself to be successful? How does the Lord measure success?

REJOICE IN TRUTH

Love does not delight in evil but rejoices with the truth.
1 CORINTHIANS 13:6 NIV

God's truth cannot be denied. The world tries to blur the lines on what is evil and what is good, but if we know the Word of God, the truth is very evident. God's Word is not subjective. It does not change due to our feelings or desires.

When sin is painted in such a way to appear appealing, or it is coated with a fake mask of religiosity, we have to cling to the truth. True love for God and his people will insist on the truth, regardless of how prominent or attractive evil acts are.

I rejoice in your truth, oh God. I delight in your love and in your presence. Evil and wrongdoing cannot distract me from worshipping you because it is empty and misleading. Even if the sin masquerades itself as truth, I will not be swayed because you have given me your truth. You fill me with joy and with hope, and I am fully yours.

Have you ever felt compelled to cheer for evil or find delight in it? What was the motivation of your heart?

EXALTATION

Be still, and know that I am God.
I will be exalted among the nations,
I will be exalted in the earth!
PSALM 46:10 ESV

This psalm is not an invitation to be lazy, but to heed God. Children of God are expected to work hard, be responsible, and fulfill their duties. We are not, however, to frantically attempt to force our way through life ourselves, without heeding the Word of God or accepting his help and intervention.

When we rely on the power of our own strength, the temptation is to exalt ourselves. God is our source of strength, and he alone is to be exalted in the earth. He may choose at times to honor us as a good father does, but we should be glorifying him and recognizing his leadership in our lives.

Still my mind, Father God, and teach me to patiently and quietly listen to you. Relieve the pressure I feel to do more than I ought, and help me bear my load. I am dependent on you and I exalt your name in everything I do.

Do you take time to listen to God leading you and correcting you?

GOOD FATHER

"He arose and came to his father.
But when he was still a great way off,
his father saw him and had compassion,
and ran and fell on his neck and kissed him."

LUKE 15:20 NKJV

The faithfulness of the Lord is beyond human comprehension. He is always attuned to our needs and patiently leads us despite our shortcomings. When we wander off course, he redirects us. If we rebelliously refuse him and waste his precious gifts, he waits with eager anticipation for us to return to him.

It is never too late to turn back to God. Regardless of where we are or the decisions we have made, the Lord will receive a repentant person with open arms and kisses. Heaven celebrates when we turn away from serving ourselves or others and return to our caring Father.

You truly are a good Father, and I run to your embrace. Thank you for forgiving my past, bringing me into your family, and loving me so completely. I am undeserving of your love and grace.

What did the father do for the disobedient son who returned to him?

POTTER AND CLAY

Yet, O Lord, you are our Father.
We are the clay, and you are the potter.
We all are formed by your hand.
ISAIAH 64:8 NLT

We are carefully designed for a purpose exactly the way God intended. The Lord does not make mistakes; he makes masterpieces. Before we criticize ourselves, we ought to consider the insult this is to our Creator. Rather than focusing on what we lack, we recognize instead our unique design.

While it is honorable to work toward improving our health, minds, and emotions, we should not become disdainful of who we are today. Those who have invited God to be the Lord of their life have the Holy Spirit living within them. They are his chosen temple and are precious in the sight of God.

You are the potter and I am clay in your hands. You have created me to be beautiful to you and to bring you glory. Please also teach me how to use the gifts you have fashioned me with to point back to you, my incredible designer.

Do you marvel at how the Lord formed you and praise him for your body, mind, talents, and personality?

ENCOURAGE OTHERS

Encourage one another and build one another up,
just as you are doing.
1 Thessalonians 5:11 NASB

The events of life and the digression of the world should not shock us or cause us to panic. Instead, the realization that one day we will go home to Jesus should encourage us and reassure us through the dismal times. We are called upon to share that encouragement with other believers so they too can be motivated to endure.

As we edify others, may it be with a heart that yearns to see them prosper in their life with the Lord. As each person is different, so how they become motivated will be different. We need to listen and learn from the Lord regarding his creations. Then, let us humbly serve other believers, provide them comfort, and spur them on in their faith.

Lord, thank you for walking with me and encouraging me. In turn, I look around to see who needs encouragement. I am part of your body and am committed to operating as such, since I am devoted to you. May I always be willing to build others up, assisting them to achieve their best life in you.

How can you encourage someone else today?

GOD IS GOD

God is not man, that he should lie, or a son of man,
that he should change his mind.
Has he said, and will he not do it?
Or has he spoken, and will he not fulfill it?

NUMBERS 23:19 ESV

When Balak sent Balaam to curse the Israelites, he quickly learned that the Lord had blessed the Israelites instead, and he dared not oppose the Lord. He returned to Balak and broke the news that the Israelites had the Lord on their side. No amount of cursing would succeed in harming the Israelites, for the Lord's purpose will always prevail.

As humans, we cannot see the future, nor are we always conscious of our own limitations. There are times when we can be fickle or drawn different directions by our desires. We change our minds, forget promises, and act dishonestly. The Lord is not like that; his words are sure. When God says he will do something, he always does it. He is ceaselessly honest, reliable, and steadfast.

You have always been faithful to me, even when I disobeyed you, God. You are fighting battles on my behalf that I cannot even see. Even if others were to curse me, they cannot oppose you.

How can you learn to be more like God in this matter?

UPRIGHT

The word of the Lord is upright,
and all His work is done in faithfulness.
PSALM 33:4 NASB

The Lord is not worried about how his plan will take form. He has an upright way for achieving everything he intends. He will never cheat, steal, or lie as others might when they feel pressured. He is faithful and honest in all his dealings. His ways are upright and his Word does not deceive. He is clear and upfront about what we can expect when we choose to follow him.

The way in which we conduct ourselves at home, at work, or in society should mirror the master we follow and truth we claim to uphold. Even if we feel like nobody will know the difference, the Lord is always watching us. He has shown us that there is an upright way to live in any circumstance, and we have no excuse for choosing any other route.

Lord, your ways are upright and true. Help me learn from your example and live accordingly.

Do you ever feel pressured to act in a dishonest fashion in order to achieve something you feel is worthwhile? What can you do instead to demonstrate that your trust is in the Lord?

JULY

Remember this: sin will not
conquer you, for God already has!
You are not governed by law
but governed by the reign
of the grace of God.

ROMANS 6:14 TPT

THE HEART

"Do not look on his appearance or on the height of his stature, because I have rejected him. For the LORD sees not as man sees: man looks on the outward appearance, but the LORD looks on the heart."

1 SAMUEL 16:7 ESV

We are so enamored by what our eyes can behold, rarely can we overlook completely what is visible versus what is unseen. To learn the true character of someone beyond their physical extremities takes time and intention. The Lord already knows each person entirely, for he made them. He is not fooled by first glances.

Our hearts, in which our deepest secrets hide, are seen and known by the Lord. We offer our best faces for other people, but there is no reason to put on airs for the Lord. He knows us and loves us even so.

I trust your judgement far more than I trust my own, dear Lord. You see what I cannot, and you consider matter thoroughly whereas I am bound to only my fragmented knowledge. Please give me your eyes to see people the way you do, and humbleness to accept what you have decreed.

Why did Samuel question God's choice?

LIVING SACRIFICE

I plead with you to give your bodies to God because of all he has done for you. Let them be a living and holy sacrifice—the kind he will find acceptable. This is truly the way to worship him.

ROMANS 12:1 NLT

After detailing the doctrine of faith and salvation, Paul appeals to his readers that they live a holy and surrendered life. Doing so does not in any way earn us our salvation, since it is a gift earned and given by Jesus Christ alone, but it is the appropriate response to the incredible forgiveness God has shown us.

When we were deserving of death, God gave us life and freedom. We have no life apart from him, so we offer our lives back to him in gratitude. The way we worship God is by responding to his love and calling as changed and obedient children.

Thank you for giving me eternal life, setting me apart, and allowing me to worship you with my life. I also praise you for allowing me to come just as I am, for I am already spotless in your eyes because the sacrifice you made.

Since Christ died for your sin, God sees you as unblemished and has set you apart. How can you be like a living sacrifice to him right now?

FEAR THE LORD

Those who fear the LORD are secure;
he will be a refuge for their children.

PROVERBS 14:26 NLT

A reverent and honest fear of God will oblige us to be obedient. The Lord does not want us trembling in fear, but to hold a healthy respect for his power and position in our lives. Just like parents love their children but still must demand respect and obedience, so the Lord gives us commandments so we will stay safe and mature as we ought.

Fear of the Lord keeps us out of harm's way. Rather than being seduced by sin, we dread disappointing our Father. We cling to what is good and make it our ambition to please him in all that we do. He is our refuge and we should abide by his laws since we are under his rule.

You never lead me astray, Father. Your rules are for my sake, for my safety and growth. Thank you for parenting me in love and for offering me security in your Word.

Do you fear the Lord or do you do what you want?

SELFLESSNESS

Don't be selfish; don't try to impress others.
Be humble, thinking of others as better than yourselves.
PHILIPPIANS 2:3 NLT

Unity and brotherly love are of so much higher priority than chasing our own haughty desires. We tend to care for ourselves first, and then extend to others whatever may be left of our time, energy, or provisions. How drastically this would change if we esteemed others as of higher importance than ourselves!

Paul is not condoning self-hatred or false humility, but that we care for others in the body as if they were our very own flesh, which is how God intended us to be. We tend to take care of ourselves and our household first before turning our attention outward, but God wants us to be humble and always consider others.

Lord, I am sorry for every time my own pride interferes with the way you intended me to operate. Help me to listen more than I talk and to give more than I take.

Who do you degrade, openly or privately? How would your attitude toward them change if you thought of them more highly than yourself?

CASTING CARES

Cast your cares on the LORD and he will sustain you;
he will never let the righteous be shaken.

PSALM 55:22 NIV

We have a Father who would like to help us carry our load. He is pleased to listen to our petitions, and he offers us comfort when we are distressed. It was never his intention that we should walk alone nor carry our burdens by ourselves. Rather than worrying, we are invited to cast our cares on him, for he is more than capable of handling them.

The Lord wants to see us set free and to sustain us through our journey. When we trust in him for support, we are immovable because of his faithfulness. To walk in righteousness is to rely on the Lord, for then even if the whole world trembles, we will not be shaken.

I cast my cares upon you today, God. Please relieve my heart and give me peace. Sometimes worry gets the better of me, but then I remember that you are greater than my troubles. I trust you to sustain me amid the strongest storms.

What is worrying you today?

REST

"Come to me, all you who are weary and burdened, and I will give you rest. Take my yoke upon you and learn from me, for I am gentle and humble in heart, and you will find rest for your souls. For my yoke is easy and my burden is light."

MATTHEW 11:28-30 NIV

It may seem like the Christian walk is difficult, but that does not account for the power of the one who walks with us. He is not a cruel god with lofty expectations. He does demand that we uphold certain values, but he also offers us all the help we need.

True, the path is narrow and full of danger, but it is God who leads us through and offers his protection. When we grow weary, he gives us rest. When we feel burdened, he gently lifts us up. He is a kind and modest God who wants the best for his followers.

Lord Jesus, like you, I have a cross to bear. Unlike you, I am offered rest and help when it is too much for me to carry. Thank you for your gentleness toward me and for helping me lift my burdens.

What does it mean to take Christ's yoke upon you?

REBUKE

Do not rebuke mockers or they will hate you;
rebuke the wise and they will love you.

PROVERBS 9:8 NIV

There are some who are unwilling to hear the truth. Rather than stir up trouble by starting an argument, we should simply leave those people alone. The Lord will deal with them in his time. It is not necessary or helpful to continue reproving those who do not have any intention of accepting correction, for it will only result in hatred and offense.

Save the truth for those who are humble enough to learn. Those are the individuals worthy of advice. They will return rebuke with sincere love and appreciation, for they have the godliness to understand that wise reproof can serve them greatly. They care less about winning an argument than they do about increasing in wisdom.

God, please give me the discipline to back down from a hostile conversation before it transcends to a fight. The world has enough hatred without me exacerbating it further. I trust you to deal with situations I am incapable of changing.

Are you a mocker or are you wise? How well do you accept correction?

OPPORTUNITY FOR JOY

When troubles come your way,
consider it an opportunity for great joy.
For you know that when your faith is tested,
your endurance has a chance to grow.

JAMES 1:2-3 NLT

It is important to note that James is not insisting that suffering Christians are to feel the emotion of happiness, but rather that we consider it a reason for rejoicing. Since we know God, we have an awareness that he can bring good out of a bad situation. Often, with simply this admittance, our hearts will follow where our heads lead.

Even if we are not experiencing any sort of euphoric feelings of bliss, our minds know that trials and troubles are opportunities for joy as we allow the Lord to work in us, building our faith and endurance in him.

Father God, in every trial large or small you are there willing to meet me. You have such power and love that you take things which were meant for evil and bring forth good instead. Thank you for every opportunity in which my faith can grow because I know it is your intention to leave me lacking nothing.

Can you choose to genuinely rejoice when you do not feel happy?

APPROACHING GOD

*This is the confidence we have in approaching God:
that if we ask anything according to his will, he hears us.*

1 JOHN 5:14 NIV

This verse should vanquish any idea Christians may have of God simply being a wishing well. Tossing prayers up to heaven and hoping for our own desires to be fulfilled is not how lovestruck, servant-hearted believers are expected to approach the Almighty.

When our deepest desire is for the Lord and for all people to come to know him, we pray to him for directions and answers that align with his agenda. That does not mean we have to vet our prayers or leave out details and requests that matter to us, but that everything comes under a covering of a mutual understanding that his master plan is what we are aiming at and hoping for above all else.

Your ways are not my ways, Lord, and I am grateful for that. I ask that you teach me your ways and align my heart to yours so that, when I come to you in prayer, I ask for your will to be done. Then, when you fulfil your will and my prayers, you reignite my confidence in you.

How can you learn what the will of God is, so you can pray accordingly?

SING OF STRENGTH

As for me, I shall sing of your strength;
Yes, I shall joyfully sing of your lovingkindness in the morning,
for you have been my stronghold
and a refuge in the day of my distress.
PSALM 59:16 NASB

We know the goodness of God personally because of the things which we have faced. In the midst of our distress, God remains our constant refuge and strength. If we focus on him rather than our hardships, we will clearly see that he is there with us through it all, not allowing us to fall, showing us the path to redemption.

God will not allow us to undergo more than we are capable of handling, but we were not meant to handle it alone. He is with us, so we cannot fail. If our burdens seem too big to carry, it could be that we are attempting to use our own strength rather than running to God.

I praise you, for you are good, God. Your lovingkindness constantly surrounds me, and your strength is my refuge in times of trouble. I will sing of your greatness forever, for you have filled me with joy.

How is a having a loving relationship with God a refuge?

WHAT IS REQUIRED

He has told you, O man, what is good; and what does the Lord require of you but to do justice, to love kindness, and to walk humbly with your God?

MICAH 6:8 NASB

During a hypothetical conversation between Israel and God, they ask what they need to sacrifice to compensate for their sins. Would animal sacrifices or rivers of water be enough to satisfy God? No. As God had already told them, he desired hearts that were surrendered to him.

We are to do justice, which is to act in a way that is right. Without excuse, God requires righteous behavior. Being kind and merciful is also necessary to God. He is just and also merciful, and those who claim to follow his ways should act as he does. That is the only way we can walk humbly with God. Even Jesus humbled himself to show us how, so we have no excuse as to why humility is too farfetched for us.

Oh God, your requirements are so fitting of your character. You are a fair and compassionate king who calls those in his kingdom to live similarly. No amount of extravagant religious deeds can recompense a lack of love. Thank you.

What does walking humbly with God mean for you each day?

DEAL WITH ANGER

In your anger do not sin. Do not let the sun go down while you are
still angry, and do not give the devil a foothold.
EPHESIANS 4:26-27 NIV

Anger in itself is not rebuked, but we are to exercise self-control and not allow anger to lead us to sin. God expresses anger, and yet he always does what is right. When we inevitably feel angry, it is important that we do not allow it to control us, but that we control it and learn how to understand God's heart through it.

When anger is allowed to linger, it festers and can produce bitterness. Unresolved anger gives the enemy more chances to lead our hearts astray and cause us to sin. When we feel angry, we should work it out with God, act appropriately, and leave it at the cross.

Jesus, anger can be so blinding. Please help me fix my eyes on you. I want to learn from your example of love, tempered anger, and incredible self-control.

What makes you angry? What actions can you take to channel your anger in a godly manner?

WISDOM GRANTED

For the Lord grants wisdom!
From his mouth come knowledge and understanding.

PROVERBS 2:6 NLT

Solomon may have been the wisest man to ever live, and he himself declared that it is the Lord who gives wisdom. We can learn and gain insight by our own endeavors, but true wisdom comes from God alone.

In order to become wise, we must seek the Lord. We must listen to his words, spend time with him, and obey his directions. In doing so, we are granted wisdom. Left alone to our own whims, we can only attain factual knowledge.

I seek you today for wisdom, dearest Father. Without your understanding, I can only deduce direction from human understanding. You have shown yourself to be generous, and you abundantly give wisdom to me when I ask for it and search for you.

What is the difference between God-given wisdom and human understanding?

END OF ALL THINGS

The end of all things is at hand; therefore be self-controlled and sober-minded for the sake of your prayers.

1 PETER 4:7 ESV

Every day draws us closer to the end of this world, when God will judge the righteous from the unrighteous, restore all that has been broken, and reign forever as the rightful king of creation.

Since we do not know when that day will be, the only proper response for us is to pray. Our prayers do not need to be wrought with panic since we have confidence in Christ. We also should not be living for the moment or pleasure-seeking, since we are called to be disciplined and rational.

Hear my prayers, God, and please help me to be like you. I want to be self-controlled and sober-minded. I do not want to be impulsive or chase fleeting fantasies like so many do. Make me wise as I realign my focus daily to be fixed on you.

How do you know that the end of all things is at hand? What does Peter mean?

EXTRAVAGANT LOVE

Your love is so extravagant it reaches to the heavens!
Your faithfulness so astonishing it stretches to the sky!
PSALM 57:10 TPT

This world is not vast enough to contain the love of God. Even the finality of death could not thwart God's loving plan. So extravagant is the love of Christ that he gave his life for us! The king of the universe knelt to wash the feet of his friends, so they would know how much he cared for them and so they would go and do likewise for others.

The faithfulness of God is evident in everything we see. All his promises are fulfilled or will be, and he never turns away from his people. The stars are just one example of God's faithfulness. They stretch across the sky every night, reminding us of all the wonders he has put in place for us.

Lord, you promised Abraham that his descendants would be more numerous than the stars, and they are. You made a covenant with to never flood the earth again, and you haven't. You put stars and rainbows in the sky to remind me of your faithfulness and extravagant love.

How did Christ's love bridge the gap between earth and heaven?

NOTHING ON MY OWN

*"I can do nothing on my own.
As I hear, I judge, and my judgment is just,
because I seek not my own will
but the will of him who sent me."*

JOHN 5:30 ESV

Since Jesus was one with God and knew clearly the will of his Father, he knew that his judgment was just. He was not responding to scenarios out of his flesh, or staunchly upholding religious ordeals for the sake of tradition.

In all things, Jesus heeded the voice of God and acted accordingly. He knew God's voice and will perfectly because, although he came as a man who could do nothing without God, he was still wholly one with God.

Your judgment, Jesus, was met with such opposition and scrutiny. You were not esteemed as God, and yet you continued to love your oppressors and offer them all your forgiveness and glory. I will choose to honor you, even when it is unpopular or conflicts with my own desires. May my desire be for you and for your will above my own.

What attributes of God did Jesus reveal that he also embodied?

FORGET FORMER THINGS

"Forget the former things;
do not dwell on the past.
See, I am doing a new thing!
Now it springs up; do you not perceive it?
I am making a way in the wilderness
and streams in the wasteland."

ISAIAH 43:18-19 NIV

The Lord reminded the Israelites that it was he who carved a path for them through the sea, who drowned their enemies and freed them from their slavery in Egypt. This was miraculous, but not worthy to even be compared to the redemption he had planned for their future.

Forget what God has done and focus on what he is doing: Jesus Christ is coming to offer salvation for sinners once and for all!

Jesus, you are my way through the wilderness, a refreshing stream running through the middle of a wasteland. You bring hope where there was none and refreshment to those who need it desperately. Of all God's wonders, you are the greatest. Nothing else compares with you.

How do you respond to God's provisions?

ADDING

*Because you have these blessings, do your best to add these things
to your lives: to your faith, add goodness; and to your goodness,
add knowledge.*

2 PETER 1:5 NCV

The blessings to which Peter is referring is summarized in the prior verses: we have grace, peace, and everything else we need to live a godly life because of our faith in God through Jesus Christ. We have been saved from corruption and invited to participate in fulfilling God's purposes.

So often we fail to dissimilate from the world. We have been given wonderous gifts from God, yet we do not use them. Our lives ought to reflect what we believe is true, and that means putting forth effort to obtain goodness and knowledge.

Lord, the faith you have given me awakens a desire to be good as you are good. The more I learn about you, the more I want to know you deeper. Please add goodness to my faith and knowledge to my goodness. It is not for good works or knowledge alone, but for the sake of my faith in you.

How can you do your best to add to your faith? What does that look like practically?

SUBJECT TO WEAKNESS

He is able to deal gently with those who are ignorant and are going astray, since he himself is subject to weakness.

HEBREWS 5:2 NIV

At no point in our suffering or weaknesses can we claim that God is uncaring or does not understand what we are going through because Jesus faced every adversity. He was tempted and tested in every way, yet he held fast to God and to goodness.

God's response to our pain is gentleness. When we are ignorant or heading in the wrong direction, he compassionately takes our hands and turns us back around. Jesus has so much love and tenderness toward us that he went through every trial on earth for our sake.

Thank you, Jesus, for your lovingkindness and your grace toward my shortcomings. Thank you for suffering on my behalf and for forgiving my ignorance. You are the perfect mediator.

Can you think of any instances when God reassured you of his love and grace?

ALL GENERATIONS

The Lord is good and his love endures forever;
his faithfulness continues through all generations.
PSALM 100:5 NIV

The goodness of the Lord has continued throughout all generations. He has been faithful to all who have gone before us and will be to everyone who comes after us. He was faithful to our parents and he will be faithful to our children.

God's promises are as true and attainable today as they were when he pledged them. He has not changed his mind or given up on us. His love endures forever; of that we can rest assured.

You are worthy of my praise just because you are my Creator. You are also good and loving toward me. I am your child and a recipient of your lovingkindness. I worship you willingly because you are good. You have always been good and you always will be.

Why does the Lord constantly tell his people to remember his faithfulness, tell their children about it, write it down, and erect monuments as reminders of what he has done?

WORTHY OF THE LORD

We continually ask God to fill you with the knowledge of his will through all the wisdom and understanding that the Spirit gives, so that you may live a life worthy of the Lord and please him in every way: bearing fruit in every good work, growing in the knowledge of God.

COLOSSIANS 1:9-10 NIV

Paul's beautiful prayer for the Colossians beseeched God to fill them with the knowledge of his will. He wanted the people to truly grasp and live out the will of God. This would accomplish four things in their lives.

First, they would be made wise. Second, it would result in them living in a way that was pleasing to God. Third, they would have successful ministries because people would recognize God through them. Finally, their faith and understanding of God would mature and so their faith would be strengthened.

Father, please fill me also with the knowledge of your will so I can walk in wisdom, be pleasing to you, be effective in reaching others, and be more understanding of who you really are.

How does being given the knowledge of God's will ultimately lead to the knowledge of God? What is the difference?

BLESSED TO GIVE

I have been a constant example of how you can help those in need
by working hard. You should remember the words of the Lord Jesus:
"It is more blessed to give than to receive."

ACTS 20:35 NLT

Most of us love to give each other gifts, but find it is much more challenging to give our time, emotions, affection, or provisions.

When we are busy, but we stop to help someone else in need, we are acting the way Christ would. When we desire praise and yet choose to applaud someone else's hard work rather than touting our own, God remembers. When we work hard to help someone else achieve success, the body as a whole is blessed.

Remind me, Father, of what you gave freely. Please help me to not become consumed with the things I want and miss out on the blessing of giving to others—even when it is so hard it hurts. You, after all, gave your very Son for me.

What can you give of yourself today?

CHEERFUL FACE

A joyful heart makes a cheerful face,
but when the heart is sad, the spirit is broken.
PROVERBS 15:13 NASB

Real joy is lasting and is not deterred by circumstances here on earth, for it is caused by the hope we have in Jesus for our eternity. Since it is secured in that which will not fail, it cannot be broken by anything we know to be momentary. Our joy is a gift that cannot be taken away. It helps us to find cheer when everything in our lives seems to be in disarray.

There will be times of sadness in all our lives. Each one of us will face our own tragedies. It is when we give way to sadness and allow it to dictate our condition that our spirit is broken and we can no longer find the motivation to press forward. With eternity in our hearts, we must cling to the joy that has been given to us. It will give us the strength and determination we need to overcome.

God, help me to not live downcast, but to radiate the joy I have from knowing you. Even when I have been kicked down, help me rise again, for I am not broken anymore.

What is the difference between having joy and feeling happy?

ONE BODY

Yes, there are many parts, but only one body. The eye can never say to the hand, "I don't need you." The head can't say to the feet, "I don't need you." In fact, some parts of the body that seem weakest and least important are actually the most necessary. So God has put the body together such that extra honor and care are given to those parts that have less dignity. This makes for harmony among the members, so that all the members care for each other.

1 CORINTHIANS 12:20-21, 24-25 NLT

The healthiest body is one that takes care of all its members and recognizes the value of each as well.

When we are comfortable and confident being who God made us to be, and when we support and encourage others to do the same, only then can we properly function as a body and as a well-designed team.

Lord, thank you for every member of your body! Thank you that under you I am united with other believers for a common goal. Please teach me the true value of working with others and help me to treat each person you have created with respect.

What are some skills you do not possess that you are grateful others do? What gifts do you contribute to the body of Christ?

CARRY ME AWAY

Hear my cry, O God, attend to my prayer.
From the end of the earth I will cry to You,
when my heart is overwhelmed;
lead me to the rock that is higher than I.
For You have been a shelter for me,
a strong tower from the enemy.

PSALM 61:1-3 NKJV

With all his resources and power, David still knew that the only place he could turn to for lasting comfort and assurance was God. He called on God to save him from his enemies and the anxiety of his heart. In the past, God had provided him protection, and David knew that he would do it again.

Christ Jesus is the Rock who is higher than we are. When we feel overwhelmed, depressed, or attacked, we ought to call on God to be our strong tower. The trials may not cease, but the Lord promises to preserve us through them.

God, you never promised that the rain would stop, only that you provide shelter for me. Good and bad happen to all, but rather than be tossed around by the waves of life, I have the immovable Rock to cling to.

Have you taken shelter in God, or are you still at the mercy of the elements?

JUDGMENT

"Do not judge, or you too will be judged. For in the same way you judge others, you will be judged, and with the measure you use, it will be measured to you."

MATTHEW 7:1-5

God is quick to forgive, but if we fail to extend mercy to others, the Lord will withhold his mercy from us. To thank God for his incomparable kindness, he simply asks that we do the same for others. The Lord alone is Judge; we are not worthy to assume such a role. Only God can see a person's heart and can judge a matter accurately.

Having been forgiven our debt of death, it should be a small matter to forgive others their petty offenses. In the cases when others cause us great amounts of harm, we can find help from God to overcome the matter. He will judge all things; it is not our place.

Please be kind and compassionate toward me, Lord God. I know of my own depravity, but you accepted me and saved me still. You forgave my sin and declared me acquitted. With so much forgiven, how could I not also forgive the sins of others. I will show my gratitude to you in the way I treat others.

How can you keep from judging others?

BOAST IN THE LORD

Here is what the one who brags should boast about. They should brag that they have the understanding to know me. I want them to know that I am the LORD. No matter what I do on earth, I am always kind, fair and right. And I take delight in this.

JEREMIAH 9:24 NIRV

All of our accomplishments amount to nothing if they are not for the sake of Christ. Everything apart from God will one day pass away. So, the greatest boasting we should do is in what God has done for us.

We ought to boast that we know God, for that is something to be greatly desired. When we are transparent about our life in Christ, others may want what we have found.

In everything, you are kind. All that you do is fair and right. You delight in doing good, and I can trust you indefinitely. I will boast of your true character and proclaim to others how wonderful it is to know you! May others hear my words and search for you as well.

Do you believe that the Lord is always kind, fair and right? Does what your eyes behold on earth sometimes deceive you from believing God's character?

SCRIPTURE

All Scripture is God-breathed and is useful for teaching, rebuking, correcting and training in righteousness, so that the servant of God may be thoroughly equipped for every good work.
2 TIMOTHY 3:16-17 NIV

Numerous accounts of collaborated evidence dictated by trustworthy individuals over the span of two millennia comprised the Bible. Its sacred teachings are infallible and timeless. The necessity of them and the relevance of their application has never waned since they were first passed from one generation to the next.

God not only had the power to endow select individuals to transcribe his words, but also the wherewithal to preserve them throughout the ages. It cannot be tarnished by time or translation because the one who authored it is as powerful and wise now as he always has been.

I know that your Word is true, dear Lord, and that you are dependable. Your teachings are the standard by which I base my life. Thank you for your loving rebuke, for rules that keep me safe, and for being my dependable guide always.

How well do you receive correction?

FOLLOW AND FEAR

You shall follow the Lord your God and fear Him;
and you shall keep His commandments,
listen to His voice, serve Him, and cling to Him.

DEUTERONOMY 13:4 NASB

The Lord tests the hearts of mankind to reveal whether we really love and trust him above all else. He commanded that if a false teacher were to try to persuade us to follow other gods or worship anything other than Christ, we are not to listen. Even if that speaker were to demonstrate through signs and wonders, it could be that the Lord is testing us and giving us an opportunity to choose him.

Following God means we are not worshipping anything other than him. If we fear him, we will be obedient. If we listen to his voice, we will not be fooled by mere spectacles.

I come before you in reverence today, Lord, for you are holy, mighty, and just. I follow you and reject anything which competes for your place in my heart. I will cling to you always, for you are my rock.

If God already knows the condition of your heart better than you do, what is the benefit to being tested? Who does it benefit?

SET FREE

God brought out his chosen ones with singing;
for with a joyful shout they were set free!
PSALM 105:43 TPT

The psalmist reminds us that we are to make known to everyone what God has done, to tell of his wonders, and to proclaim his name . We are quick to forget what the Lord has already led us through. By intentionally remembering what he has done, we have greater confidence moving forward. We know he is good and will always come to our aid.

Throughout the chapter, Israel was reminded of all God had done for them. He swore a covenant with them which he upheld, delivered them from Egypt, and fed them in the desert. He also called down famine and allowed them to be enslaved. His discipline may seem harsh, but it is out of love and is temporary. He will always set his people free.

I will remember your grace toward me, Lord. Instances throughout my life where you have rescued me will forever be cherished as evidence of your care. I confidently continue, knowing that you have set me free.

Can you remember specific times in your life when God has rescued you or provided for you?

CHEERFUL GIVER

Each of you should give what you have decided in your heart to give. You shouldn't give if you don't want to. You shouldn't give because you are forced to. God loves a cheerful giver.

2 CORINTHIANS 9:7 NIRV

The Lord repeatedly makes it clear that is it not the religious rituals that move his heart, but the joy his children experience from following him. He wants our hearts, not our actions. Grateful and cheerful hearts will desire to do good and live generously. At that point, it is no longer simply a Biblical obligation, but a privilege and a delight.

God has plenty of wealth. He can address every need himself, but he chooses to use us as participants in his plan. This is an honor not to be taken lightly. It should overwhelm us with gratitude and cheer.

Turn my heart toward you, Lord, and I will experience your joy by obeying you. It is a delight to give and to have the resources to bless others. What does it avail if I give but my heart is bitter? Teach me to give from my heart.

How does giving benefit the giver as well as the receiver?

AUGUST

God still loved us with such great
love. He is so rich in compassion and
mercy. Even when we were dead and
doomed in our many sins, he united
us into the very life of Christ and
saved us by his wonderful grace!

EPHESIANS 2:4-5 TPT

STRENGTH AND INSIGHT

To him belong strength and insight;
both deceived and deceiver are his.

JOB 12:16 NIV

Job's friends told him that if he were truly blameless, God would not allow travesty to befall him. They preached that those who do God's will have laughter put in their mouths. Job argued that this is not always the case. He knew he was innocent, and yet the Lord had allowed terrible suffering to befall him. Job pronounced that all strength and insight come from God, and he rules both the good and the bad.

Suffering is not a sign of sin. To suffer and still abstain from sinning is pleasing to God's heart. We will have tragedy in this life. Pain inflicts the unjust as well as the just. The Lord does not promise us laughter. But one day our suffering will be over. Until that day the Lord is close by to help us.

I do not pretend to know better than you, Lord God Almighty. Everything you do is done in love. When I suffer, may it increase my faith. Rather than rejecting you, help me cling to you.

How can you continue to trust God when you are suffering?

BEAR THE WEAK

We who are strong ought to bear with the failings of the weak and not to please ourselves.

ROMANS 15:1 NIV

The context of the direction Paul is giving to believers who are stronger in their faith is when sin is not specifically the issue, but rather topics which are vague or culturally influenced. Earlier, Paul addressed issues such as eating meat, drinking alcohol, or celebrating questionable holidays. If someone weaker in the faith feels compelled to act a certain way, it is better for them to abstain rather than go against their conscience.

It is also better for those who are more mature in their faith to support those who are weaker in their journey of understanding the Lord rather than obnoxiously revel in their freedom in front of them. Although the Bible may not ask us to abstain from certain things, our abstinence may be necessary since the faith of our brothers and sisters is more important than our own pleasure.

Rather than judge or challenge others who are wrestling through where they stand on extra-Biblical principles, Lord, please give me the patience and insight to support and encourage them. I want to stand together with them rather than offend and divide.

Can you think of a time when you laid down your own rights for the sake of another?

STRAIGHT PATHS

*Trust in the L*ORD *with all your heart*
and do not lean on your own understanding.
In all your ways acknowledge Him,
and He will make your paths straight.

PROVERBS 3:5-6 NASB

As we prudently plan our lives, it is important to remain attentive to God's voice and submissive to his better way. We can have such assurance, knowing that God is with us throughout our lives. He keeps us going in the right direction and never leaves us to stumble about in the dark.

Our own understanding can only take us a short distance, but God's guidance will take us all the way home to him. We only need to acknowledge and accept him.

Lord, you have an understanding and a viewpoint that I do not, so I put my faith in you and trust that you will lead me down the straight path. When I encounter obstacles, I will look to you for direction. Also, when my days are easy and the road is clear, I will still turn to you in all things.

Why does the Lord want you to acknowledge him before straightening your paths?

ANY CIRCUMSTANCE

Not that I speak from want,
for I have learned to be content
in whatever circumstances I am.
PHILIPPIANS 4:11 NASB

Contentment is not a natural response to being without; it is a mindset that is learned from relying on God. When we undergo seasons of being in need, we learn more intimately how fulfilling God is and how faith in him is really what carries us through the most challenging times.

Rather than turning to worldly answers first, we should learn contentment and trust. When circumstances cannot steal our contentment because of our confidence in God's care, it fills us with true joy and peace.

God, please teach me contentment in all things. Whether I have plenty or I am in need, you remain the same. You are always good, always loving, and always fully in control. Please guide me as I work hard and trust you with the outcome. I want to be responsible without worrying about the future because I know you are in control and you are always faithful.

How can you practice contentment today?

JOY OF THE RIGHTEOUS

May the righteous be glad and rejoice before God;
may they be happy and joyful.

PSALM 68:3 NIV

God did not come from us; we came from God. Our sole purpose is intermingled with our service to him. He has given each of us a calling, and it is our delight to learn to walk the path he has put us on. So then, unlike others who may scramble for fleeting happiness, we have true joy in doing the work of the Lord.

We rejoice in God because he satisfies our souls. Our longing and our loneliness fade away and are replaced with joy and contentment. As God's righteous people, it is our both our mandate and our gladness to follow the Lord's commands.

To walk in righteousness brings me true joy and delight, Father, for I love to worship you. I want to worship you with my life. Thank you for giving me a purpose and a calling and filling my heart with gladness.

Does obedience still give you joy even if you do not want to obey?

COLD WATER

"If anyone gives even a cup of cold water to one of these little ones who is my disciple, truly I tell you, that person will certainly not lose their reward."

MATTHEW 10:42 NIV

After Jesus called the disciples to himself and gave them authority to cast out demons and heal the sick, he told them to go out and proclaim his message. They were not to carry provisions with them, but to rely on the help of others. Jesus decreed that anyone who helped them would never lose their reward. He always sees and always blesses us when we love others, especially those who are in need.

In the same way, we ought to be humble enough to receive help from others. The Lord is always faithful to us, and he likes to use people to support each other. Part of being a member in the kingdom of God is caring for one another. That means giving care and receiving it.

God, show me the people you would like me to support, so I can truly give of myself. As I learn to serve you with others, unite us and show me specific ways I can help.

How can you help those who are proclaiming Christ's message?

GET WISDOM

The beginning of wisdom is this: Get wisdom.
Though it cost all you have, get understanding.
PROVERBS 4:7 NIV

Wisdom comes from God alone, so in order to grow in wisdom we must seek God. Wisdom is different than mere intelligence or knowledge; it is having the mind of Christ. Wisdom supersedes common sense and even intuition. It is of higher value than anything the world boasts of.

If our entire lives were spent in the pursuit of wisdom—truly, the pursuit of God—they would be lives well spent. No amount of riches or fame is worth surrendering our search for wisdom, and understanding its value is the first sign of a wise person. Although it may take everything we have and cost us greatly in other areas, following God and becoming wise is worth more than everything else.

Oh Father, you are so wise and understanding. The wisdom you possess is far above mine, and I can only marvel at your magnitude. I love to spend time with you, to learn from your lessons and find encouragement from your words. Please increase my wisdom, so I can also teach and encourage others.

What might you have to surrender to further your pursuit of wisdom?

SACRIFICE OF PRAISE

Let us offer through Jesus a continual sacrifice of praise to God,
proclaiming our allegiance to his name. And don't forget to do
good and to share with those in need. These are the sacrifices
that please God.
HEBREWS 13:15-16 NLT

After being encouraged to hope for heaven rather than becoming overly anxious about worldly things, the persecuted Jews were told to offer a continual sacrifice of praise to God. The Lord no longer demands animal sacrifices for sin since Jesus paid for our sins on the cross. Now, he simply desires praise from his people.

Two ways of praising God and thanking him for restoring our lives is by remaining faithful to him and by helping those in need. The Lord dearly loves the needy, and when we care for them it is as if we are directly caring for him. Pompous and self-proclaiming religious acts do not impress God, but those who are faithful and extend love and service to others is greatly pleasing to him.

Lord, you are so loving that what you ask for in return for your grace is that I love others. Thank you for paying for my sin. I will praise you continually with my life.

Who do you know in need? What do you have that you can share?

ABIDE

*We have come to know and have believed the love which God has
for us. God is love, and the one who abides in love abides in God,
and God abides in him.*

1 JOHN 4:16 NASB

Both knowing God and believing in God is essential for
the life of a Christian. One can believe that God is who he
says he is, and yet not have a personal relationship with him.
Similarly, one may love the attributes of God, yet doubt his
deity. Acknowledging God's supremacy and ultimate rule is
necessary, as well as fostering a growing relationship with him.

True sacrificial and genuine love is the trademark of a
believer. God is love. Love originated with him and was
perfected by him. If we truly believe this and know him
personally, he will abide in us, and we will be loving because
we serve the God of love.

**Oh God, thank you for loving me. Thank you for authoring
love and sharing it generously with your creation. May I be
so filled with your love that it pours out onto my family,
friends, communities, and anyone else you bring into my life.**

How can you abide in God?

STEADY HEARTS

They won't be afraid of bad news;
their hearts are steady because they trust the LORD.
PSALM 112:7 NCV

None of us like to receive bad news, but we do not live in dread of it like those whose security is shaky. Our hope is rooted in our steadfast Lord, and our confidence comes from knowing him. We cannot secure our own futures nor the results of certain circumstances. In the end, we know the final conclusion of all things is our victory through Christ.

God knows the future and has a perfect plan in place. He is not surprised by sudden disappointments; he has been preparing us to handle them. For this reason, we do not live in fear but in freedom. Our hearts are steady because we trust God, and he has given us his peace.

Father, my heart knows peace because I know you. Although I do not know what lies ahead of me, I know you and that is enough. You are faithful and loving to me always, so even bad news cannot unravel my faith.

Does your heart feel steady or anxious thinking about what you cannot predict or control?

LOVERS

My lover is mine, and I am his.
SONG OF SOLOMON 2:16A NLT

The Lord gave himself fully for us, and he asks that we do the same. The previous verse warns the Shulamite woman of the little foxes who will ruin the vineyard of love if she does not catch them. These little foxes are all the distractions in our lives that ruin our relationship with God. Any selfish desire which positions itself between us and the path God has for us threatens to trample on our love.

We are God's beloved children. Just as Solomon and the Shulamite women cherished each other, so God cherishes us and desires the same passion from us. Marriage itself is a picture of how Christ loves us. That is how we are to love one another and how God wants to be loved. We are his, and he is ours.

The way you pursue me and love me is both humbling and compelling. There is nothing else worthy of your place in my life. Indeed, I am nothing and have nothing apart from you. I love you and give myself fully to you.

Do you have any little foxes that need catching?

WORK FOR THE LORD

*Work with enthusiasm, as though you were working
for the Lord rather than for people.*
EPHESIANS 6:7 NLT

Our attitudes matter because they reflect the conditions of our hearts. No matter what our situations are, we are to wholeheartedly work as if we were serving the Lord directly.

Paul wrote this to the Christians in Ephesus from prison or house arrest. He did not allow his unfortunate and unfair circumstances to steal his joy or deter him from encouraging others. He served God and that was evident in his attitude.

God, I am sorry for every time I express a complaining or contemptuous attitude. I know that, ultimately, my work is for you and my attitude reflects my love for you. My work is a form of my worship to you.

How can you respond to unfair work conditions in a just way that is still honoring to God?

TIMELY WORDS

A person finds joy in giving an apt reply—
and how good is a timely word!
PROVERBS 15:23 NIV

An appropriate word given at the right time is very beneficial both for the giver and the receiver. To obtain the sort of wisdom this requires does not come in a sudden burst of insight, but rather from quietly listening to God.

We do not suddenly become the answer during the situation. God has the answers, and we can only give them to others by learning from him. In meekness, we should hold back our own words and ask God what he would like to tell others through us.

As I fill my heart with you, God, please fill my mouth with your words. You see all things, including the hidden struggles of others. Use me to speak encouragement and truth. Keep me from spouting off my own words and teach me to listen for your leading and insight.

Have you ever received a word that was so fitting at such an opportune moment that you knew it had to be wisdom from God that inspired it? How did that make you feel?

LIFTED UP

Humble yourselves under the mighty power of God, and at the right time he will lift you up in honor. Give all your worries and cares to God, for he cares about you.

1 PETER 5:6-7 NLT

The longing for significance is something intrinsically woven into each of us. The Lord does not reject the exaltation of humans, in fact he often exalts his faithful followers, but it should not be our focus. By serving God with humility and grace, we forego our pursuits of self-glorification and put our effort toward praising God's name.

In the most suitable time and in the most appropriate way, God will raise us up if we relinquish that role to him. We were uniquely made for a God-given purpose, and his plan for our lives is so much greater than anything we can conjure up on our own.

Humble me, oh Lord, and overwhelm me with your grandeur. I want to glorify you and serve you with my whole heart. I surrender my own desire for exaltation to you and focus instead on your adoration.

Do you publicly flatter yourself, hoping for praise or recognition? Is God's approval enough?

HIGHWAYS TO ZION

How blessed is the man whose strength is in You,
in whose heart are the highways to Zion!

PSALM 84:5 NASB

The ancient Hebraic form of writing often presented literal and figurative pictures side by side. Zion, or Jerusalem, is where the temple of God stood. People walked a long highway to get there, so desperate were they to be in the presence of God.

David recognized that true strength is cultivated through a loving relationship with God and a heart bent on being in God's presence. They are so deeply in love with him it is as if the highways to Zion, or the paths into God's presence, are in their own hearts. We no longer have to travel to a distant temple to go before the Lord, for we have the Spirit of God present with us.

My heart searches for you, Lord God, and clings to your every word. Without you, I am lost and weak. With you I have direction, purpose, and strength. It is you who makes me strong enough to endure the journey, and it is your home I journey toward.

How far are you willing to go to be in the presence of God?

TRUE DISCIPLES

*"If you abide in my word, you are truly my disciples,
and you will know the truth, and the truth will set you free."*
JOHN 8:31-32 ESV

Being a disciple of Christ entails more than simply admitting his lordship. A true disciple responds to divine discipline. As followers of Christ, we are to live by his words and hold fast to his truth. The truth can seem offensive at times since it is often contrary to our human desires.

Many will turn back from following Christ when it means they have to let go of their own agenda, but what devoted disciples will come to realize is that true freedom is only found in the message that Jesus Christ brought.

Lord Jesus, I pray against offense and surrender my agenda to you. I will choose the path less trodden and carry my own cross like a true disciple. Every day, I will abide in your Word so I will know the truth and not be manipulated by the enemy's lies.

What are some examples of sins that disguise themselves as freedom but are just lies?

NOT ASHAMED

Fear not, for you will not be put to shame;
and do not feel humiliated, for you will not be disgraced;
but you will forget the shame of your youth,
and the reproach of your widowhood you will remember no more.
ISAIAH 54:4 NCV

When Israel was enslaved by the Babylonians, they not only lost their freedom but their dignity as well. They felt disgraced. In those days and within that culture, a woman who could not conceive a child was shamed by her community. God likened the humiliation Israel felt to that of a barren woman. He promised to rescue them not only from the Babylonians but from their own humiliation as well.

When the Lord sets us free, we are completely free. He breaks our bonds of sin, forgives our past, and rescues us from death. He also blots out our shame and humiliation. They no longer have any dealings with us, and we need to leave them at the feet of Christ.

Because of you, I am no longer ashamed, Lord Jesus. You have taken away my guilt and shame, and you remember them no more. Help me also let go of my past mistakes and forgive myself, since your work of forgiveness is full and complete.

Do you still feel guilty for things you did in your past? How can you surrender your guilt and be free?

GOOD EXAMPLE

In every way be an example of doing good deeds. When you teach, do it with honesty and seriousness. Speak the truth so that you cannot be criticized. Then those who are against you will be ashamed because there is nothing bad to say about us.

TITUS 2:7-8 NCV

We can say whatever we want, but who we are is reflected in our actions. If we promote honesty and then lie, we clearly do not promote honesty. Our good deeds declare our testimony much louder than our speech does. That is why it is so important that what we say is not contradicted by how we act.

The world is watching and listening, and those who oppose Christ will look for cracks in our message. We cannot be perfect, for only Christ is perfect, but we can live honestly and sincerely. Insisting on living honorably and respectfully will disprove any accusations people hurl against us.

Your words are true, Lord Jesus, and your way is pure. I want to walk in your way and speak your truth. Please shine light on any wicked or dishonest ways that are within me and bring them to light so I can correct them.

What opportunities do you have to speak truth today?

HOLD ONTO HOPE

Let us hold unswervingly to the hope we profess,
for he who promised is faithful.

HEBREWS 10:23 NIV

Christians were being persecuted and pressured to return to Judaism which denied that Jesus Christ was the true Messiah and God Almighty. Those early believers knew that Jesus' words were true and his lordship real. He was faithful and they could not be unfaithful to him.

At every turn, this world attempts to make us question the faithfulness of God and the deity of Jesus Christ. Lies are often intermingled with truth so they are harder to recognize and easier to swallow. When we hold fast to the hope of Jesus which we have acknowledged to be true, we can have full confidence because we know the Lord is faithful.

God, your plan is far greater than mine. Since the start of creation, you have set in motion your great mission to save me from my sin. Thank you for your grace, for sending Jesus to pay for my wrongdoings, and for being faithful to me no matter what.

What is the hope mentioned in this verse?

FAITHFUL FOREVER

Praise the Lord, all you nations;
extol him, all you peoples.
For great is his love toward us,
and the faithfulness of the Lord endures forever.
Praise the Lord.

PSALM 117:1-2 NIV

Although this is the shortest psalm in the Bible, its impact is still immense. Within this brief lyrical are four chief components. It is first prophetic, a foretelling of God's plan that one day every nation will praise him. It further reveals that the Lord is eternal, as is everyone he is faithful toward, including us.

The psalm testifies of who God is; how loving and faithful he is. In response to his greatness, it instructs us to praise him. The Lord is faithful forever, and by his great love he has saved anyone from any nation who is willing to give their life to him. The application of this abundant grace is appropriate: praise him!

Lord, your heart is so loving and your faithfulness so enduring that you have invited all the nations of the earth into your family. By your greatness, forgiveness and family is offered to all. Still, you know me by name and cultivate a relationship with me. I praise you, dearest Lord!

Rather than singing along with prescribed lyrics, can you write down personal reasons why the Lord is praiseworthy to you?

APPROACH GOD

In him and through faith in him we may approach God
with freedom and confidence.

EPHESIANS 3:12 NIV

The access we have to approach God in prayer comes from Christ's sacrifice for our sins. We have been made pure and clean, so we can freely approach him. The confidence we have to come before him is because of our faith in Christ's sacrifice for us. He died for us, purified us, established our faith, and invited us to approach God.

None of what God did for us was by our merit, it is our free gift of salvation and means we have relationship with our Savior. We can only choose to respond and embrace it.

As I come before you in prayer, heavenly Father, I recognize that even this right is a gift from you. Thank you for breaking down the divide between me and you. I praise you for the freedom and the confidence you have filled me with. How blessed I am to serve a God who desires a relationship with his creation.

Do you have confidence in Christ? How do you know?

GOD IS FOR US

What then shall we say to these things?
If God is for us, who can be against us?
ROMANS 8:31 ESV

Paul is once more writing to persecuted Christians who were no strangers to pain and suffering. When Jesus was on the cross, he experienced the weight of God abandoning him as he took the payment for our sins on his own body. Because of this, God promises never to abandon us. The penalty for sin has been completed.

We may suffer many things in this life. At times we may feel lonely, but this is just a feeling. The truth is that we are never alone. God is for us, and there is nothing that can stand against us.

God, regardless of how I feel, I will remember your truth and acknowledge that you are always there for me. In the suffering I undergo, the sins I commit, and the loneliness I sometimes feel, you are still with me and nothing can come between us.

Do you believe that God is for you?

GUARD YOUR HEART

Above all else, guard your heart,
for everything you do flows from it.
PROVERBS 4:23 NIV

Throughout verses 20-27, Solomon warned that we should keep close watch over our ears, mouths, eyes, and feet. But above all, he cautioned us to guard our hearts. We may be able to fool people with our mouths and our feet for a time, but eventually the condition of our hearts will pour out. It is from our hearts that everything else flows.

If our hearts are fixed on what is good, our ears, mouths, eyes, and feet will be inclined to do what is good. Since everything we do points to the condition of our hearts, our first priority should be submitting them to the Lord.

Help me guard my heart, for I long to bring honor to you, God. I am not disciplined or strong enough to always control my actions without the help of your redeeming love. Please change me to want what you want, and guard me from anything attempting to attack me.

What does guarding your heart look like within the culture today?

GROWING UP

When I was a child, I used to speak like a child,
think like a child, reason like a child;
when I became a man, I did away with childish things.
1 CORINTHIANS 13:11 NIV

The process of spiritual maturity is simply that: a process. Christ has each of us on a journey to understanding him better, and we are to put aside our childish ways and embrace his teachings. We cannot be fully mature, understanding all that we should, until Christ comes back and shows us all things.

In the meantime, he has left us his Holy Spirit to guide and teach us and has given us spiritual gifts for the purpose of edifying each other.

How I long for the day when you will return, Lord Jesus! My mind will be fully renewed and my eyes will behold your glory. I want to know you as you truly are. Until that day comes, please keep sanctifying me. I want to be spiritually mature, put aside childish things and pursuits, and serve others with the gifts you have given me.

What are some childish things you would like to put aside?

ABUNDANTLY MERCIFUL

You, Lord, are good, and ready to forgive,
and abundant in mercy to all those who call upon You.
PSALM 86:5 NKJV

The Lord is good and everything he does is good. The Lord is forgiving and merciful toward everyone who asks him. The obvious conclusion is that forgiveness and mercy are good. Forgiveness is not always earned or even requested, but it is godly and expected of us nonetheless.

Nobody has suffered greater offense than God. There is no one who has undergone worse mistreatment than our perfect Lord and Savior. If he is willing to forgive those who ask, and he shows them mercy by pardoning them, then we have no qualifying reason why we cannot align our hearts with his and extend forgiveness as well.

You are abundantly merciful, heavenly Father, and you have forgiven me so much. I know that all your ways are good, and so I will follow your example and exchange a desire for vengeance with a heart willing to extend mercy.

Is there someone you need to forgive?

LOVE YOUR ENEMIES

"Love your enemies! Do good to them. Lend to them without expecting to be repaid. Then your reward from heaven will be very great, and you will truly be acting as children of the Most High, for he is kind to those who are unthankful and wicked."

LUKE 6:35 NLT

The Lord's character is unchanging, regardless of whether he is dealing with someone submitted to him or someone bent on destruction. If people steal from us, attack us, or are in any form unkind, it is still up to us to be generous, peaceful, and loving. The true intent of the matter and the condition of our hearts is not between us and them; it is between us and God.

Because God loved us, we can and should love our enemies. If they never repay us for our love and generosity, we can rest assured that the Lord repays. We are not counted among the wicked, we are children of God. In so saying, we ought not mirror their mistakes, but resemble our Father in heaven.

Help me love those who do not love me back, Father. I am your child, and I will insist on following your ways. In you, all is made right in the end.

How can you love your enemies?

IT WILL HAPPEN

From the beginning I told you what would happen in the end.
A long time ago I told you things that have not yet happened.
When I plan something, it happens. What I want to do, I will do.
ISAIAH 46:10 NCV

God does not expect us to be cluelessly led around by blind faith. Although many things have not been revealed to us yet, from the very beginning God explained what would happen to us in the end. He has not hidden his intentions from us; in fact, he invites us to be active participants in his plan.

When God says he is going to do something, we can have complete faith that he will do what he said. Our hope is sure. One day we will be with God in glory. He told us in the beginning that was his plan for us, and by his great faithfulness it is still his plan today.

I read your Word and realize that all your promises are true. Everything you have told me you will enact. My faith in you is not displaced, for you are an honest God who loves to be known by his people.

Why did God tell his people his plan from the very beginning?

FULL UNDERSTANDING

*May the Lord lead your hearts into a full understanding
and expression of the love of God and the patient endurance
that comes from Christ.*

2 THESSALONIANS 3:5 NLT

In asking God to lead or direct the hearts of the
Thessalonians, Paul used the Greek word kateuthynai
which means to remove all obstacles. He wanted anything
that hindered their pursuit of God's love and their patient
endurance to be stripped away.

In the moments we feel like we are being stripped down
to nothing, or we do not have what we think we need to keep
going, we can remember that Christ has given us a patient
endurance and the Lord wants to guide our hearts into a full
understanding of himself. To truly know God means to truly
experience love. Let nothing stand in the way of you and him.

I do ask, Father, that you remove from my life anything that
distracts or hinders me from pursuing you with my whole
heart. Your love is worth more than anything this world can
offer.

*Is there anything standing in the way of you fully
understanding God and his great love?*

GRACIOUS GOD

He passed in front of Moses, proclaiming,
"The LORD, the LORD, the compassionate and gracious God,
slow to anger, abounding in love and faithfulness."

EXODUS 34:6 NIV

While the Lord was revealing himself to Moses and bestowing on him the ten commandments, the Israelites were at the base of the mountain worshipping a golden calf. They had erected the calf because they grew tired of waiting for the Lord. Although this disappointed God, it did not stop him from teaching them and pursuing them.

Unlike the Israelites and so many of us, the Lord is faithful and slow to anger. He does not give up on his people but continues to show them compassion and grace. There were consequences for the Israelites behavior because the Lord abhors sin, but his love for his people continues to abound.

You are far more gracious than I am, Father God. Even though you knew your people would be unfaithful, you made a covenant with them which you have always upheld. Thank you for your faithfulness toward me. Forgive me when I am unfaithful.

How can you thank God for his faithfulness today?

TODAY

The Lord has done it this very day;
let us rejoice today and be glad.
PSALM 118:24 NIV

The conditions Psalm 118 were written in were very bleak. The psalmist shared about the destitution of his position. With enemies surrounding him and feeling as if he were about to fall, he still wrote that we should be glad and rejoice. Joy is a choice; one we must make in the good times as well as the hard times. It requires action and decision. Our perspective must be bigger than our problems, and our hearts need to stay fixed on God.

By his grace and faithfulness, the Lord has created every day. This alone is reason to thank him and to rejoice. The days belong to the Lord whether they are full of happiness or travesty. We can choose to be grateful and glad, regardless of what we have to face.

You made the day today, and I praise you for it, God. The way you lead me through hardships and into your presence is outstanding. Please keep me from becoming so overwhelmed by the problems I face that I forget to rely on your grace to see me through.

What about today makes you glad?

IMAGE OF CHRIST

We all, who with unveiled faces contemplate the Lord's glory,
are being transformed into his image with ever-increasing glory,
which comes from the Lord, who is the Spirit.

2 CORINTHIANS 3:18 NIV

When Moses witnessed the Lord, his face shone with a brightness so pure it was unbearable to the other Israelites who had become hardened in their sin. Similarly, the Lord intends for us to be his reflection to the world. Light uncovers dark places and is often uncomfortable to people who want to hide.

The Lord searches for every hidden heart, and he has chosen to use us by shining through us. The way in which we behold God's glory is not through good works or study but when God removes the veil separating us and shines his face upon us.

Shine your light on me and through me, Father God. May darkness flee from your presence. Even if you send me out into dark places, I know that you go with me and dwell in me, so darkness has no power over me. Only you can make the night shine like the day.

How do you see God's light shining in and through you?

SEPTEMBER

The LORD is
compassionate and
gracious, slow to anger,
abounding in love.

PSALM 103:8 NIV

BRAVERY

*Be courageous! Let us fight bravely for our people
and the cities of our God. May the LORD's will be done.*

2 SAMUEL 10:12 NLT

David sent condolences to the new king of the Ammonites upon his father's death. Suspicious of David's motives, the new king humiliated David's messengers which enraged David. Both sides prepared for battle. David appointed Joab to lead the army, however the Arameans had joined the Ammonites in the battle. So, Joab deployed half of the army under his brother Abishai, while he led the other half.

Joab instructed his brother that if one of them realized they were overpowered, the other must come to the rescue. Then he commissioned him with the words from this verse. When fighting for the Lord, we should be brave! We fight for the sake of others with the Lord as our leader. We never need to fight alone.

God, may your will be done in my life. Help me to have courage to do what is right, and to fight for the sake of others. Please give me friends who I know I can count on in the midst of life's battles.

Who do you know you can depend on to come to your rescue if you need it?

LIVING PEACEABLY

*If possible, so far as it depends on you,
live peaceably with all.*
ROMANS 12:18 ESV

We can have more impact on others for Christ if we choose to love and live peaceably rather than standing staunchly in our ideas. When Daniel and his friends were instructed to defile themselves with food God had told them not to eat, instead of insisting on the right way and suffering the consequences, Daniel humbly asked that they be given the opportunity to try things God's way first.

By choosing a peaceful approach, Daniel's faith had a much further influence. As followers of the Prince of Peace, we should strive to live peaceably with everyone whenever we can.

Dearest Jesus, when you offered this world peace, it was met with a sword and a cruel death. You lived peaceably whenever you could. There were times that called for your hand of punishment instead, but you always do everything in love. Thank you for that and for being my example.

What should you do when your attempts at peace are rejected?

SELF-CONTROL

Better to be patient than powerful;
better to have self-control than to conquer a city.
PROVERBS 16:32 NLT

To what benefit is it to conquer a city if the other city had better intentions? If the Lord were to select someone to do a job, would it not make more sense that he chooses the one who is willing to listen to him and patiently wait for his instructions over the one who is more powerful?

Our power and our strength come from God as does our calling. Enacting skills he has given us brashly and arrogantly is unfitting for a child of God. He has equipped us in order to obey him. Therefore, having self-control and patiently waiting upon the Lord's instructions is of more worth than spoils from an entire city.

Lord, I wait patiently before you. Teach me to be cautious and controlled. Even if others are running forward in life and conquering all sorts of cities, I will follow your guidance and remember that it is never about my glory. Thank you for the power you have given me. Please teach me to use it on behalf of you.

Have you asked the Lord how to use your skills and talents?

SINCERE AND BLAMELESS

This I pray, that your love may abound still more and more in real knowledge and all discernment, so that you may approve the things that are excellent, in order to be sincere and blameless until the day of Christ.

PHILIPPIANS 1:9-10 NASB

Love is one of the key elements of the Christian faith. It must, however, be coupled with knowledge and discernment. Knowing God and understanding his heart is where true love comes from. He is the creator of love and so understanding him is how we are filled with love.

Discernment also comes from an awareness of what God wants. Discerning love can serve with purpose and show care in a way that is helpful rather than perpetuating problems. Both these attributes cause our love to go deeper and abound even more, but they can only be attained through an active relationship with God.

Lord, please cause my love to abound as I seek to know you more. I want a living and active relationship with you that is established in love. Please fill me with knowledge and discernment so I am able to love others to the best of my ability.

What excellent things is Paul referring to in this Scripture?

MAKE HIM KNOWN

*I will sing of the lovingkindness of the Lord forever;
to all generations I will make known your faithfulness
with my mouth.*

PSALM 89:1 NASB

During a time when problems were paramount and the attacks on David's dynasty seemed to never cease, Ethan penned the words of the beautiful Covenant Psalm. Throughout their troubles, the mercies of the Lord became clear to David's kingdom. Ethan could have complained about all the turmoil they had endured; rather, he chose to praise God for his lovingkindness and his faithfulness.

We may feel like complaining eases our pain but recognizing the Lord's faithfulness in the middle of a terrible situation does far more for our attitudes. Grumbling turns quickly to gossiping and can spread negative feelings. Thanking God for his provision and protection fills us with joy, and that is far better.

God, when difficulties fall upon me, rather than complaining about my plight, please help me see it as an opportunity to recognize your lovingkindness in my life. Nothing can befall me that you will not preserve me through. I choose to glorify you and tell everyone of your goodness and your grace.

How can you see the loving hand of the Lord at work in your life today?

RECEIVED

"He who receives you receives Me,
and he who receives Me receives Him who sent Me."
MATTHEW 10:40 NASB

In the ancient world, a person's family was their identity. When travelling, people would go to other family members and expect to be welcomed. Even if the relatives did not personally know them, they would accept them on behalf of their parents. Who someone was had everything to do with what lineage they came from.

When Jesus commissioned the believers to go out into the world and share his message, he reminded them that they came from him. He was calling them family. Since we are all in the family of God, we are expected to accept and support each other as relatives. We should embrace other believers, and especially those who are sacrificing to do Christ's work. In doing so, we are welcoming God as well.

Father, to realize that you have not only accepted me as your child but also proudly stand by me in the world is both honoring and humbling. I want to be a good representative of you, ready to receive other family members as I also welcome you.

In what practical ways can you receive or welcome those who have been sent by God to share his message?

SECURITY

The LORD is your security.
He will keep your foot from being caught in a trap.
PROVERBS 3:26 NLT

The Lord encourages us to search matters out and to learn his ways. He also has grace on us, and does not condemn us for not understanding all things. We have his written Word accessible to us, yet we have not fully grasped all its content. The Lord, therefore, guides our steps and guards our hearts against the attacks of the enemy.

The devil lays traps for us, and sometimes we fall into them. Our heavenly Father is our security, and by his grace he helps us to avoid these snares or lifts us out of them. We all stumble in many points, and none of us understands the Scriptures fully. We must lean on Christ for security and not on our knowledge. He alone can carry us through danger to safety.

Humble my heart, Lord, to receive your help and accept your correction. Guide me around the enemy's traps and guard my heart against his attacks. His lure is everywhere, but I will choose to focus on you instead.

What things make you feel secure?

FATHER OF LIGHTS

Every good gift and every perfect gift is from above,
coming down from the Father of lights
with whom there is no variation
or shadow due to change.

JAMES 1:17 ESV

Every good thing in our lives is from God. There is a danger in concentrating too much on what we lack, challenging God's goodness with questioning why he hasn't given us more.

The truth is there is beauty in learning contentment. God's goodness doesn't change, regardless of our circumstances. He wants the best for us, blesses us abundantly, and at times refrains for our own good and growth.

Thank you for all your good gifts, Father God. Thank you for life both now and into eternity. Thank you for the people I love the most intimately. Thank you for sending Jesus to save me. When I catch myself complaining about what I do not have, please remind me of everything you have gifted me with.

Other than obvious gifts, what are some smaller gifts that God has blessed you with?

WORTHY

You are worthy, our Lord and God, to receive glory and honor and power, for you created all things, and by your will they were created and have their being.

REVELATION 4:11 NIV

Within the vision God gave to John, he saw twenty-four elders before the throne of God. They were declaring the truths written in this verse. From God alone and for God alone do we exist and have a purpose. We are not an accident or an afterthought.

Creator God designed this world with all its wonder because it was his will. It is his will that we live, and he is therefore worthy of the praise of our lives. All glory, honor, and power are his, for we are nothing without him.

May you receive the honor you are due, Almighty God! I want my life to demonstrate the gratitude that I feel. You created me and you gave me meaning. I love to uncover your purposes and declare your praises, for it is why I was made. Nowhere am I happier and more myself than before you.

What do you think your main purpose in life is?

TAKE REFUGE

It is better to take refuge in the Lord
than to trust in people.
PSALM 118:8 .NLT

It is easy to run to other people for help and advice: those we can see with our eyes and hear with our ears. A closer relationship with God will lead to understanding how he is the one we should be running to first. God has put other people in our lives so we can support and encourage each other, but he alone has all wisdom and power.

The Lord is a mighty refuge that can ease your worries and help you overcome your obstacles. Instead of only wanting immediate answers from human sources, we should be cultivating a habit of patiently and faithfully seeking God first, then waiting for his response.

The more I seek you, Lord, the more obvious it becomes to me that there is no substitute for your presence. With you, I am safe and sure. Thank you for the people you have put in my life. Help me to appropriately recognize that they are only my support and not my source of saving grace.

How has the Lord provided you refuge when people couldn't?

MAKER

As you do not know the path of the wind, or how the body is formed in a mother's womb, so you cannot understand the work of God, the Maker of all things.

ECCLESIASTES 11:5 NIV

Our Father loves to reveal his handiwork to us. He created this world for our enjoyment and exploration. But there remain mysteries that are beyond our comprehension. As our technologies advance, we begin to uncover more of God's intricate creation only to realize that there is still infinitely more we do not know.

God loves to be understood, sought after, and marveled at. We can understand that because he placed the same desires in us. It is incredible to consider that this powerful God does know us intimately. The one who created this whole world finds us beautiful and desires us above all else.

You are such a creative, mighty, and exciting God. I love to learn more about you and the wonders you have made. Thank you for surrounding me with such beauty, and creating it all for my pleasure. I am left speechless knowing that of all the amazing works your hands have fashioned I am what you love the most.

What in creation has left you in awe of God?

SUBMIT

Submit to one another out of reverence for Christ.
EPHESIANS 5:21 NIV

Submission does not mean passively following along with everyone else. To submit within the context being given means to put the needs of others above our own. We can do this because we revere Christ.

Jesus not only put our needs above his own, he called us to do likewise. Then he promised to take care of all our needs. Because of this, we have an example to follow and an assurance that God will always be with us ready to care for our every need.

Sometimes, Jesus, I am so blinded by my own plight that I fail to recognize the battles others around me are facing. Please open my eyes to view the needs of others and open my heart to put my priority into helping them. No matter what, I know you will take care of me and that equips me to take care of others.

How can you submit to others out of the respect you have for Christ?

DO NOT STRAY

Let not your heart turn aside to her ways;
do not stray into her paths.
PROVERBS 7:25 ESV

The difference between the Proverbs 31 woman and the Proverbs 7 woman is that the former learns from God and lives to serve others while the latter learns from her culture and lives to please herself. The Proverbs 31 woman blesses many by her hands, but the Proverbs 7 woman destroys those around her.

If the attention we seek comes from the world, then our actions and words will speak of it. The attention we should seek is attention from God, for his opinion is the one that matters. Praise and affirmation from men will never satisfy us because our contentment can only be found in the one who designed our hearts.

Guard my heart, Lord, and teach me how to be praiseworthy. I want your approval and will not cater to the whims of my culture. Teach me to be modest and respectful in heart as well as appearance, for I seek to serve you and others rather than myself.

What messages does your culture tell you that contradict what the Bible teaches?

NEIGHBORS

*You were called to freedom, brothers. Only do not use your freedom
as an opportunity for the flesh, but through love serve one another.
For the whole law is fulfilled in one word: "You shall love your
neighbor as yourself."*
GALATIANS 5:13-14 ESV

The difference between a worker who only wants to do the
bare minimum and a worker who loves to work is everything.
We have been given freedom and grace, yet the true measure
of our hearts will be revealed in how we choose to embrace
our freedom.

Simply knowing we will always be forgiven should not
entice us to indulge in whatever lifestyle we desire. Someone
who has truly been changed by the love of God will desire
to serve him and show him love in return. We do this by
upholding his commandment: to love God and love others.

**God, today I want to choose to use the freedom you
generously gave me as an opportunity to serve others
and show them the love you have filled me with. On your
behalf, I will love others because I am so overwhelmed with
love for you.**

*Why does Paul say the whole law is fulfilled in loving your
neighbors as yourself?*

COVERING

He will cover you with his feathers,
and under his wings you will find refuge;
his faithfulness will be your shield and rampart.

PSALM 91:4 NIV

Like a bird shields its young from the elements, so God covers us. His faithfulness is our defense. His desire is to gather us to him just as a hen gathers her young, but so often we would rather try to find our own way. A baby bird is not equipped to venture out into the world on its own; it needs the protection of a loving mother. When danger comes, it can run for safety into her arms.

Similarly, when we face perilous situations, we can run into the loving arms of God, for he will cover us and take care of us. Even if we were to attempt something in our own strength, God hovers over us ready to catch us when we fall and teach us how to soar with him again.

Lord, cover me with your grace and protect me from all evil. I know that it is your strength and faithfulness that sustain me, and by no merit of my own.

How has God's faithfulness shielded you in the past?

PEACE GIVEN

"Peace I leave with you; my peace I give you.
I do not give to you as the world gives.
Do not let your hearts be troubled and do not be afraid."
JOHN 14:27 NIV

In many cultures people will bid each other peace before parting. Jesus spoke these words to his disciples before his crucifixion and departure back to his Father. It was not, however, just a well-intended salutation but an actual promise.

The disciples were about to enter a time of great persecution, but Jesus promised he would leave them his peace, which he did in the form of the Holy Spirit. When they faced terrible persecution, they did not have to be afraid because Jesus' peace was greater than anything the world could offer.

Thank you for your peace, Lord Jesus. I know that I am never alone and never need to be afraid. Your Spirit gives me strength and your kingdom is one of peace and love. When you give a gift, it is sure and eternal.

Is your heart troubled by something? How can you receive Christ's peace?

PRAISE

I will tell about the LORD's kindness and praise him for everything he has done. I will praise the LORD for the many good things he has given us and for his goodness to the people of Israel. He has shown great mercy to us and has been very kind to us.

ISAIAH 63:7 NCV

Those who have been truly impacted by the love of God cannot help but share the experience. Just as someone who is newly in love desires to mull over their newfound romance, so someone who has experienced what life with God is like wants to talk about it.

Recognizing the good things God has done for us and praising him for them is both honoring to God and helpful for us. It reminds us of whose leadership we follow. God's mercy and his kindness should be remembered.

I praise you, Lord, as I remember the mercy and kindness you have shown me. You have blessed me with so many good things, and I love serving you.

Can you think of some of the good things God has done for you?

NOT SLOW

The Lord is not slow in keeping his promise, as some understand slowness. Instead he is patient with you, not wanting anyone to perish, but everyone to come to repentance.

2 PETER 3:9 NIV

The false teachers pestered Peter about Jesus' promise to return. Peter simply reminded them that the same God they were mocking destroyed the world with a flood and was planning fire for his next judgement of the earth. The Lord will assuredly judge the world again, and he will keep every promise he has made. He waits because he loves us and wants to give every single opportunity for people to accept his love and repent.

We can trust God's timing because he always acts in the most loving way possible. He is the perfect blend of justice and mercy. Rather than doubt his promises, we should thank him for giving this grieving and rebellious world just a little bit more time to turn back to him.

Father, I know that you are coming back to judge the world, and I praise you for taking my guilt and declaring me innocent. I ask for the hearts of my loved ones and for all who are still lost to their sin to see the light and repent. Thank you for your patience on their behalf.

Who would you like to pray for today?

TIME OF NEED

Let us then approach God's throne of grace with confidence, so that we may receive mercy and find grace to help us in our time of need.
HEBREWS 4:16 NIV

We do not serve a distant god who cares only about our obedience and allegiance. Our God cares about our well-being and wants a loving relationship with each of us. He welcomes us to approach him and amply supplies us with whatever we need.

Without reservation, he shows us mercy and grace. When we are weak, rather than rejecting us he helps us. In our times of need, we can confidently run to him because, just like a loving Father, his arms will be wide open to receive us.

God, please help me reject any notions that you are displeased with me or disinterested in me. Your Word testifies of the pleasure you find in me and of how near you are to the broken-hearted. Even when I am embarrassed or ashamed, I know I can always run to you.

How does God respond to your needs and weakness?

PEOPLE OF INTEGRITY

Joyful are people of integrity,
who follow the instructions of the LORD.
Joyful are those who obey his laws
and search for him with all their hearts.

PSALM 119:1-2 NLT

It may seem that following a lifestyle contrary to God's instructions will bring joy and satisfaction, but it will not. Our hearts were crafted to desire God. Even if it is the more difficult option with less immediate gratification, following God gives us true fulfillment. We embrace our purpose when we choose to follow God rather than our own whims and ambitions.

People of integrity are known for being honest, dependable, and self-controlled. They are not led around by cultural pressures; they are devoted to God's instructions which give them a framework to follow. The Lord's laws give them joy because they long to serve him with their whole hearts.

God, help me live with integrity not just when it is easy but when it is difficult too. Be my deepest desire so that nothing can distract me from pursuing my true calling of worshipping you.

What Biblical values do you struggle to uphold?

CONTROL YOUR THINKING

Let the peace that Christ gives control your thinking,
because you were all called together in one body to have peace.
Always be thankful.

COLOSSIANS 3:15 NCV

When conflict arises, rather than avoiding or retaliating, we should have a mindset of peace. Christ is the one who brought peace, and since we are united under his lordship, we allow peace to govern our thinking. When we have a disagreement, we should take active steps to pursue peace.

Just as important as living peacefully is being thankful. Considering what Christ has done for us, and continues to do for us, we ought to be filled with gratitude. Such an attitude will infect how we live, think, and treat others.

My precious Prince of Peace, thank you for being the light in a dark world. Regardless of the decisions other people make, you always insist on humbly doing what is right. Please help me to be more like you.

How can you let peace control your thinking so that when conflict arises you are already prepared to handle it properly?

ONE VOICE

May the God of endurance and encouragement grant you to live in such harmony with one another, in accord with Christ Jesus, that together you may with one voice glorify the God and Father of our Lord Jesus Christ.

ROMANS 15:5-6 ESV

By God's grace, we press on. This life is wrought with difficulties and our own perseverance will at some point expire. God's grace has no end. He will always offer us the endurance and encouragement we need.

Often, God's mode of communication is through other believers. This is one more reason why it is so vital that we live harmoniously together, pursuing peace and having grace. Just like when we're singing a song with others, we each have our own part but we blend voices to sing together with one united voice.

As one voice of praise, united in Christ, assembled with others for your glory, I will worship you, God. Thank you for helping me to endure, finding strength and encouragement from those around me.

Why does the Lord want you to learn to sing with others instead of just performing a solo?

FRIEND AND BROTHER

A friend is always loyal,
and a brother is born to help in time of need.
PROVERBS 17:17 NLT

True friendships are often revealed through adversity. When the excitement wears off and the trials hit, real and loyal friends will remain to help fight the battle. Their love is constant and not dependent on what they are receiving from the relationship. Friendship does not need to be fair where true love is present.

Family may have conflict, but a good family will always help a member in need. Christ is the perfect example of a brother and a true friend. His love is constant: never wavering and eternal. He came to earth to help those in need and gave his entire life to serve those he loved. In Christ, we are family.

Jesus, thank you for staying loyal to me, even in the midst of such great torment and even when I was disloyal to you. You have loved me since before time began, and you will love me for all eternity. Teach me how to love like you.

Are you a loyal friend to those in need?

STAND FIRM

Be on guard. Stand firm in the faith.
Be courageous. Be strong.
And do everything with love.
1 CORINTHIANS 16:13-14 NLT

In summary of all Paul had written to the Corinthian believers, he recapped his letter in an almost bullet point fashion. We must stay on our guard and keep vigilant because we have a real enemy who desires for us to fail. The devil will try to tempt us and distract us from the call God has placed on our lives. The way we can distinguish lies is by standing firm in our faith and knowing what God says.

Our courage and strength come from God. He is mighty and will always save us, so we do not need to be afraid. The more intimately we know God, the braver and stronger we will be. Everything can be done in love because God is love, and those who follow God will walk in the way of love.

God, please help me in my faith, courage, strength, and love. Keep my eyes open and my heart inclined to your voice.

Why is love more important than any other commandment or any other spiritual gift?

SING PRAISES

I will sing of lovingkindness and justice,
to you, O LORD, I will sing praises.
I will give heed to the blameless way.
When will you come to me?
I will walk within my house in the integrity of my heart.

PSALM 101:1-2 NASB

David made a vow to God that he would lead his kingdom and his household with integrity. He wanted to praise God for his new position and enact lovingkindness and justice like he had learned from God's rule. Although David's desire was still to be with God in his eternal kingdom, he strove to lead his own kingdom in a way that would honor the heart of God.

Each of us can lead our own hearts and households with the same integrity, love, and justice. We have God's model to follow, and we have the Holy Spirit's help when we mess up.

In everything I do, let my life be a praise to you, my Lord and King. Lead me by your lovingkindness so I can in turn lead others in integrity.

What is the blameless way?

GOOD MEASURE

*"Give, and it will be given to you. A good measure, pressed down,
shaken together and running over, will be poured into your lap.
For with the measure you use, it will be measured to you."*
LUKE 6:38 NIV

Often, this verse will be quoted in reference to money
or tithing, but the context of Christ's meaning is in regard to
forgiveness. Prior to this passage Jesus instructed that we are
to be merciful because God shows us mercy. He said we are
not to judge or condemn, otherwise God would judge and
condemn us. Then he told us to forgive, and that in the same
measure we give, it would be given back to us.

Forgiveness is not an option. The debt God removed from
us far outweighs anything anyone else could possibly owe us.
We have been forgiven all. How can we withhold forgiveness
from others?

I praise you for your forgiveness, Father, for your grace
has set me free! Help me walk the path of forgiveness
toward others. I want to be wise and discerning, but not
withholding grace and love from anyone.

Is there anyone you have not forgiven?

UNSEARCHABLE THINGS

Call to me and I will answer you
and tell you great and unsearchable things
you do not know.
JEREMIAH 33:3 NIV

The Lord loves it when his people call out to him, for he is ready and eager to include us in so many of his wonderous mysteries. He desires an active relationship with his children so much that he sent Jeremiah as a prophet to relate his messages and draw his people back to himself.

Modern scientists continue to discover natural phenomena. There are so many more wonders and secrets that God has not revealed yet within nature about his character and that pertain to his future plan. He wants to share all these things but only with those who want to listen.

I readily run to you and listen, dear Lord, for I yearn to hear about all your unsearchable things. I have so many questions and you have so much you want to tell me. Teach me how to hear you above the noise of this world.

What questions do you have for God?

USELESS ARGUMENTS

Remind everyone about these things, and command them in God's
presence to stop fighting over words. Such arguments are useless,
and they can ruin those who hear them.

2 TIMOTHY 2:14 NLT

Paul reminded the Ephesians more than once to stop bickering over words. His lessons were meant to draw the Ephesians closer to Christ, not create a division over the irrelevance of specific phrases. If we are united under Christ, we should not allow differences to create division.

We need to be guarded against useless arguments that ruin friendships and harm others in the faith. Arguing over words could entail different versions of Scripture, for instance. The Bible teaches us to love. It does not say to allow false doctrine, but it does rebuke its readers for bickering over meaningless details.

Father, I pray that you remind me of your love and the price you paid to bring me into your family any time I open my mouth to confront another child of yours. Help me to listen carefully to you so I know if what I am saying is relevant for faith and for the gospel or if it is petty bickering.

Do you find it difficult not to argue your point? How can you choose to let your opinion go unheard?

STRENGTH AND COURAGE

*Be strong and courageous! Do not be afraid and do not panic
before them. For the LORD your God will personally go ahead of you.
He will neither fail you nor abandon you.*

DEUTERONOMY 31:6 NLT

Moses bequeathed leadership of Israel to Joshua in the presence of all the people. He commanded them all to be strong and courageous. If God was on their side, they could not be overcome. Victory would be the Lord's and all strength was his.

When we are confronted with problems too immense for us to handle, we need to ask ourselves if fighting is what the Lord wants us to do. If it is, then he will go before us and provide a way. There is no need for fear or panic when we are following God. He will never abandon us and his plans will never fail.

God, give me strength and courage to follow you no matter what dangers stand in my path. You are stronger than my enemies, and you are bigger than my fears.

Have you ever confronted an obstacle seemingly too difficult for you to overcome, and yet conquered it by God's grace?

COMMANDMENTS

I am a friend to anyone who fears you—
anyone who obeys your commandments.
PSALM 119:63 NLT

Mutual interest is bonding. We share a connection with those who strive for the same things we do. The fear of the Lord leads us to wisdom, and wise people will surround themselves with other wise people. Those who fear the Lord will do their utmost to obey his commandments. Their lives will reflect a desire to honor God.

If we also fear the Lord and strive to obey his Word, our decisions will complement each other's, and a friendship will be natural. There is a camaraderie born out of sharing a common goal, especially when that goal ties us together as family under Christ.

I have the highest respect and appreciation for you, oh Lord, and my lifelong endeavor is to obey your Word. Bring me companions who share the same values, who also want you more than anything else. May we be a source of strength to each other.

Who walks with you in striving to obey God's commandments? How can you encourage them toward godly living?

OCTOBER

The LORD waits to be gracious
to you; therefore he will rise up
to show mercy to you.
For the LORD is a God of justice;
blessed are all those
who wait for him.

ISAIAH 30:18 NRSV

RULER OVER ALL

LORD, the God of our ancestors, are you not the God who is in heaven? You rule over all the kingdoms of the nations. Power and might are in your hand, and no one can withstand you.

2 CHRONICLES 20:6 NIV

Jehoshaphat king of Judah received word that an army was coming to wage war. Frightened, his first move was to inquire of God what should be done. The Lord reassured him that he would not have to fight this battle. He directed the king and all his people to march down to where the army would meet them and witness firsthand the deliverance of God.

The next day when they arrived, all their enemies had been annihilated, and there was so much plunder it took them three days to collect it all! When we rely on God's leadership, turn to him first, and follow his commandments, he will fight our battles and overwhelm us with blessings.

God, there is none who can stand against you, for you are King over all creation! I will follow you, no matter the cost.

What battles do you need to let God fight for you right now?

NOTHING CAN SEPARATE

Can anything ever separate us from Christ's love? Does it mean he no longer loves us if we have trouble or calamity, or are persecuted, or hungry, or destitute, or in danger, or threatened with death?

ROMANS 8:35 NLT

Looking around at this world, we could ask why God would allow things to happen if he truly loved us. The truth is that God loves us enough to carry us through all things, which are here as a result of sin. He rescued us from the grip of death and bound us to him by Christ's love.

There is nothing that can ever come between us and God's love. We must remember what he has done and is doing for us rather than become dismayed at the darkness around us.

Dearest Jesus, thank you for delivering me from every form of evil and for shining your light in the darkest places. I know that there is nothing that can change who you are or how you feel about me, so I cling to you in confident hope.

Have you surrendered your fears to Christ?

HUMILITY

Humility is the fear of the Lord;
its wages are riches and honor and life.
PROVERBS 22:4 NIV

If we spend our whole lives pursuing riches and honor, we will never know the abundant life that accompanies true surrender to the Holy One. Love of self leads us down a dissatisfying path. Fear of the Lord teaches us to walk in humility, to serve rather than be served, to lay ourselves down, to take up our cross, and to follow Christ whatever the cost.

In doing so, we will experience true life the way God created it. Life spent with God is always endowed with riches and honor. They may not be in a manner the world recognizes, but heaven will declare it.

Father, teach me to be humble. So great is your majesty that I become instantly familiar with my own humanity. I trust you and desire your will far more than I trust myself or care to live for my happiness only. I want your eternal riches far more than I desire things of this world.

What sort of riches does the Lord bestow on the faithful and the humble?

LIFE IN CHRIST

If there is any encouragement in Christ, any comfort in love, any participation in the Spirit, any affection and sympathy, complete my joy by being of the same mind, having the same love, being in full accord and of one mind.

PHILIPPIANS 2:1-2 ESV

The cause and effect outlined in these verses speak to the relevance of the love of Christ and, as consequence, Christian love. Christ is our encouragement and his love comforts us. The Holy Spirit guides us and is involved in our lives. Anyone who has accepted Christ as their Savior is well acquainted with his affection and sympathy.

The next verse relates the clear outcome of such moralities: we will experience joy, love, and have a similar mindset as other believers which unites us under Christ.

This letter was written to the Philippians so long ago, and yet the same truths are evident in my life today, God. I praise you for being the completion of my love, joy, and unity.

If being in full accord and of one mind with other believers is a natural result of the love of Christ, why is there division in the church?

GOD'S GOODNESS

From your kindness you send the rain
to water the mountains from the upper rooms of your palace.
Your goodness brings forth fruit for all to enjoy.
PSALM 104:13 TPT

If the mountains, which are the highest reaches of the earth, are watered and there is fruit enough for everyone, that would mean the Lord sent enough rain to satisfy the mountain and have the remainder trickle down onto the rest of the world. Not only does the Lord supply for the mountain's needs, but for the needs of the entire world.

This is hard to realize when many places on earth suffer from poverty and malnourishment, but the Lord's provisions are eternal and not just for our temporary lives. Sin and self-interest have created a mess across the globe, but the Lord extends his grace like rain to everyone everywhere so that all may enjoy his goodness and have life eternal.

Thank you for your provisions, dear Lord. Thank you for raining on the strong mountain, and for growing tender fruit. Your supply is more than enough, and you eagerly share all you have with your children.

How has the Lord shown you kindness today?

CHRIST'S COMPASSION

When he saw the crowds, he had compassion on them, because
they were harassed and helpless, like sheep without a shepherd.
MATTHEW 9:36 NIV

Jesus does not despise our weakness. He is well acquainted with incapacities and has made arrangement for them through his death and resurrection and through giving us the Holy Spirit. When we come to him in whatever state we are in, he has compassion on us and steps in to lead us like a loving Shepherd.

When we feel stressed or lost, we should not wait to get ourselves in order before seeking Christ. In the middle of chaos, in the middle of our sin, we can seek Jesus and he will answer. He will have compassion on us and lead us back to the right road.

Lead me, Lord Jesus, and bring me back to your path. Without you, I wander helplessly around, stuck in my sin and confused at what to do. You clear away the confusion and lead me to the safety of your pastures again.

How has Jesus shown you compassion in your weaknesses?

SEARCH CONTINUALLY

I will show my love to those who passionately love me.
For they will search and search continually until they find me.
PROVERBS 8:17 TPT

In our quest to discover God and find answers, we must not give up. The Lord is always nearby, ready to love and take care of us. Sometimes he lingers so we can also show him love. He yearns to be loved in the same way he created us to desire love. By allowing us time to search for him continually and to passionately love him, we enter an active and mutual relationship.

Searching for God at any expense demonstrates a passionate love, unlike we have for anything or anyone else. It is as if we discover the greatest treasure, stop whatever else we are doing, and put all our might toward uncovering it.

God, I love you with a passionate love and I want to never cease pursuing you. You are my greatest desire, and nothing can come between you and me. Your love gives me new life and fills me with hope and joy. I praise you for you also never stop pursuing me.

In what ways have you searched for God this week?

STRIVE FOR PEACE

Pursue peace with everyone,
and the holiness without which
no one will see the Lord.

HEBREWS 12:14 NRSV

As important as peace is in the life of a believer, equally important is holiness. None of us are capable of attaining holiness on our own because our natures are prone to sin. That is why God sent the Holy Spirit to help us in our weaknesses. He equips us to handle all of life's challenges with the strength and power that comes from God. When we succumb to sin, it is a rejection of the help the Holy Spirit offers.

Sometimes even with the contribution of the Holy Spirit to our walk, we choose to sin. We are imperfect and unworthy. But when Christ died for our sins, we were made perfect and holy. The blood of Christ purified us and made us able to stand before God.

Lord, I acknowledge that I am lost without your grace. By your sacrifice alone, I am made holy. Now, I choose to walk out in holiness and strive for peace with others.

Why does your spiritual growth necessitate your pursuit of peace with others?

FELLOWSHIP

If we claim to have fellowship with him and yet walk in the darkness, we lie and do not live out the truth.

1 JOHN 1:6 NIV

Our lives are consistent with our beliefs. It is not our good works which save us, but someone who has truly been saved will reflect it in the way they live. If nothing has changed in the way we act and we continue to sin, we have deceived ourselves if we believe we walk with God.

This understanding does not permit us to cast judgement on others, since it is the Lord alone who can know the condition of someone's heart. This also does not mean we will be freed from temptation or rid of sin in an instant. God has grace on us while we are being sanctified.

Knowing you and having fellowship with you, God, redeems my heart and mind. I no longer live for myself because I have found one who is so much greater. Thank you for walking with me and bringing me forth into the light.

How are you sanctified?

UNITY

How good and pleasant it is
when God's people live together in unity!
PSALM 133:1 NIV

Unity is not something that just happens on its own. Unity requires work, humility, and openness. We can coexist without intimacy, denying the existence of issues among us, but that is not truly a unified body.

The Bible teaches us how to live peacefully with others, so it is vital that we take its lessons to heart and apply them to our lives. One of its main themes is how we ought to serve others first and put their needs above our own. This principle opposes the world's chant that you should do whatever makes you happy. If we all lived according to our own happiness, we would have billions of contradictory goals. United under Christ, we have one goal, and that is to love and serve him together.

When you saved me, not only did you give me your love and eternal life, but you also gave me a family across the globe of others who love you and who I will share eternity with. As incomplete people, we often say and do things we shouldn't. Please help me forgive others and continue to strive for unity.

If a conflict arises between you and another person who honors God, what should you do?

PLANS

"For I know the plans that I have for you," declares the LORD,
"plans for welfare and not for calamity
to give you a future and a hope."

JEREMIAH 29:11 NASB

The Israelites had been carried into exile: out of their promised land of Jerusalem and into Babylon. In response to their captivity, the Lord delivered them a letter through the prophet Jeremiah. He said to remain in the land, settle down, live among the heathens, and prosper. He promised to deliver them in seventy years, but in the meantime, they were to make the most of their captivity.

We like to imagine that this verse excludes us from pain and suffering, promising only a future full of health and happiness. It was not the case for the Israelites, and it is not for us today either. In this world, we will suffer. Suffering is synonymous with following Christ. What our gracious Lord does is takes our pain and makes something beautiful out of it.

God, your plan is often not easy, but it is good. You are working all things together for good whether I see it or not.

Why do you think God allowed the Israelites to remain in Babylonian captivity for seventy years?

FREEDOM

He is so rich in kindness and grace that he purchased our freedom
with the blood of his Son and forgave our sins.

EPHESIANS 1:7 NLT

What a tremendous price Christ paid to cover the cost
of our sins. He is worthy of our adoration and our allegiance
because it is only through him that we have life anew. He set
us free from the claim our sin had on our lives. His kindness
and grace are unfathomable, and his love continues to guide
us every step we take.

By his blood, we can truly live in freedom. Even when we
stumble, we can stand back up and keep pressing on because
he has forgiven us completely.

Your amazing grace, dear Lord, has provided me a way to
join your family and become your child. You paid a great
price for me, and I gratefully accept your grace. Thank you
for being my Father and for redeeming me.

How are you using the freedom that Christ has allotted you?

WINNING BACK

*A brother who has been insulted
is harder to win back than a walled city,
and arguments separate people
like the barred gates of a palace.*

PROVERBS 18:19 NCV

It takes much more strategy to win back an offended friend than it does to tear down a wall. The natural reaction of someone who is hurt is to recoil. When someone in close relationship with the offender suffers insult, the wound is much deeper.

We care about the opinions of those we are close to much more than we care about what strangers think. So, we are often much nicer to complete strangers than we are to our dearest family members and friends. We should be careful with our words, trying to keep from insulting those around us—especially those we are close to.

Guard my mouth from insult and unkindness, dear God. When I do insult others, help me to pursue them and earn their favor once again. I know that you made me to live in unity with my sisters and brothers, and that I am to pursue peace when at all possible. Fill me with your peace and humility, God, as I work on winning back broken relationships.

How can you win back an insulted friend?

RESPECT

Show respect for all people:
Love the brothers and sisters of God's family,
respect God, honor the king.
1 PETER 2:17 NCV

God's commandments may at times be difficult, but they are simple and easy to understand. Peter did not include any exceptions when he said that all people are to be shown respect. As Christians, we do not respect people because they are respectable but because we represent Jesus who died for the unworthy.

We are to love other believers. Again, they are not exempt if they are difficult to love, for our attitudes are modeled after Christ's. Love is not simply a feeling but an act. Respecting God is of utmost importance because by doing so we remember and acknowledge his power and supremacy. Finally, we are also called to honor those in authority over us.

Give me grace, dear God, to always treat others with respect. Even when other people are not being respectable, loving, or honorable, I will remember that I represent you, and that means I need to show them respect.

How can you honor your authority if you disagree with them? Why is this so important to do?

OFFERING

*What can I offer the Lord
for all he has done for me?
I will lift up the cup of salvation
and praise the Lord's name for saving me.
I will keep my promises to the Lord
in the presence of all his people.*

PSALM 116:12-14 NLT

The word salvation here in the original text is plural. The psalmist is not referring to the futuristic work of Christ on the cross but all the abundant ways the Lord saves and preserves us throughout our lives. What can we offer as a token of thanks for his grace? The very lives he has redeemed.

We did not create life, and we do not have the power to sustain it. The authority of life and death is in God's hands alone. Let us praise him for saving us with the way we choose to live our lives.

God, no offering I can give is worthy of your grace, but I will give you my life as a praise offering anyway. I want to live for you rather than for myself and serve others the way you taught me to do.

In what ways has God saved you in addition to Christ's ultimate sacrifice?

IN HIS ARMS

*He took them in His arms
and began blessing them,
laying His hands on them.*
MARK 10:16 NASB

The term blessing here comes from the Greek word eulogeo, which means either to celebrate or to consecrate. Whether we are parents or we take care of other children, we recognize that there is no way for us to perfectly protect and provide for them alone. Only God has true power and authority over their lives, so we have to consecrate them to him and trust that he cares for them even more than we can.

Jesus lived by example, and he has asked us to follow in his steps. He prioritized children, celebrated them, and even used them in his mission. Children are not a burden to Jesus but a blessing that he embraces. We can trust him with the children in our lives.

Father, you truly love your children. I can learn from your example and recognize how highly you value little ones. Please remind me of how valuable they are to you so I never take them for granted.

How can you value the life of a child today?

CROWN OF JOY

Those the LORD has rescued will return.
They will enter Zion with singing;
everlasting joy will crown their heads.
Gladness and joy will overtake them,
and sorrow and sighing will flee away.

ISAIAH 51:11 NIV

When the Lord rescued the Israelites out of Babylon and led them back to their own land, Jerusalem, there was great rejoicing and singing! Their sorrow was replaced by joy, for they had served in captivity for a long time. It was not the first time God had rescued them from slavery; Egypt was still fresh in their history. It also will not be the last time the Lord will rescue his people and lead them to their promised land.

When the Lord returns for his people again, we will finally enter his eternal promised land. Our sorrow and crying will be forever replaced with everlasting joy and singing.

Thank you, Lord, for never forgetting your people. You have always made a way for your children to follow you, and you always return for them when they go astray. I eagerly await your final return, and the day I go home to you forever.

Why do you think the psalmist refers to joy as a crown?

FULFILL THE LAW

Carry each other's burdens,
and in this way you will fulfill the law of Christ.
GALATIANS 6:2 NIV

Immediately after Paul instructed the Galatians to step in when someone was caught in sin and restore them, he told them how they are to do that: help carry their burdens.

Sin is cumbersome, messy, and we do not like to get our hands dirty. When a sister or brother is struggling, the best way for us to help restore them out of their sin is to step in and shoulder some of the burden they are carrying.

Give me your eyes and your love, dear Jesus, to see past the sin to the hurting person buried beneath. You did not run and hide from sin, but embraced the sinner, accepted their repentance, and washed them clean with your forgiveness. You purposefully sought out the weak and the sick to show them love and grace. Help me to do the same and so fulfill your law.

Do you know someone right now who is carrying a heavy burden? How can you help them carry it?

PATIENT ENDURANCE

Patient endurance is what you need now, so that you will continue to do God's will. Then you will receive all that he has promised.

HEBREWS 10:36 NLT

The letter of Hebrews was written to the Jewish Christians of the early church who were being persecuted for their faith in Jesus Christ. Even amid persecution, God always provides a way to do the right thing. There is never an excuse for sin. What the Christians then needed was not deliverance from their trials, but patient endurance.

Those of us who do God's will can find the strength to continue through faith, and we will receive all the blessings he has promised. We are not guaranteed an easy life, but we are assured that God's way is the only way that leads to life.

Lord, please give me patience and endurance. I want to be free from my difficulties, but my first desire is to serve you and love you with my whole heart. I know that my suffering is never in vain, for you work everything for good both for me and for your kingdom.

What do you need patient endurance for today?

WONDERFULLY MADE

I praise you because I am fearfully and wonderfully made;
your works are wonderful, I know that full well.
PSALM 139:14 NIV

The Father created us in his image for his purpose with much care and consideration. We should be careful not to complain about the handiwork of God, but to praise him for his wonderful design. He is worthy of admiration not resentment and criticism.

Taking care of ourselves can be a way of respecting God for his gift but rejecting the wonderful way he made us by hating who we are is unappreciative. We should consider how the Lord delights in us and how he created us for his pleasure.

Dear God, help me have a respectful and thankful attitude about myself. Rather than comparing myself to others, give me your eyes to see the way you do. Help me revel in my unique and wonderful design, giving you all the glory and praise.

Do you seek to improve yourself out of contempt for the way you were made or out of care for what God has given you?

YOUR BEST WORK

Whatever you do, work heartily, as for the Lord and not for men, knowing that from the Lord you will receive the inheritance as your reward. You are serving the Lord Christ.

COLOSSIANS 3:23-24 ESV

When our work is difficult, mundane, or thankless, we can remember that everything we do is for the Lord. Out of appreciation and love for him, we embrace every day's tasks with joy because we serve the King!

Even if our toils are for a difficult boss or unappreciative children, our callings come from God and our rewards do as well. We ought to put our best effort into our daily grind, even if it seems to be devalued here on earth because it has always been for God and not for mere man.

God, even when others attempt to destroy my efforts, undermine my work, and steal my success, I will continue to serve with my whole heart because that is how you called me to act. The end results are in your hands. I trust you to bless my work. You are my reward.

How has the Lord called you to serve him today?

DIFFERENT GIFTS

In his grace, God has given us different gifts for doing certain things well. So if God has given you the ability to prophesy, speak out with as much faith as God has given you.

ROMANS 12:6 NLT

Of what benefit is it if someone were to give a child a gift, but that child never opened it or used it? God has given each of us natural abilities, talents, and spiritual gifts. He wants to teach us how to use them and what they are for. With the faith that we have, he asks us to step out in our gifts. In time our faith will grow.

Imagine if the child who received the gift only wanted to play by himself. God's great plans for giving gifts includes serving and encouraging the entire body of believers. He has given each of us a special position in his family and the tools we need to play our part well. Our gifts are not for us alone but to be used to help others.

Thank you for giving good gifts, Father. Please teach me how to use them to glorify you and encourage others.

Do you have the faith to step out and use your gifts? How can they bless others?

WISDOM IS PLEASING

Know that wisdom is such to your soul;
if you find it, there will be a future,
and your hope will not be cut off.
PROVERBS 24:14 ESV

Wisdom is likened to the honey spoken about in the previous verse. Honey is sweet and enjoyable, it carries many health benefits, and it does not spoil with time. Wisdom also provides many benefits to the one who obtains it. If we are disappointed in life or feeling hopeless, pursuing wisdom can change our lives. When we seek God and gain his perspective, we will be wiser. Then, we can begin to see things as they really are.

With wisdom, we have pleasure knowing that we are serving God's purposes. We have hope for the future and for the fulfillment of God's promises.

Show me the way to wisdom, Lord. Your Word says that its worth is immeasurable and that you love to give it generously. I will seek you and your ways. Please satisfy me with yourself.

How is wisdom pleasing if your circumstances do not change?

LOVE ALWAYS ENDURES

Love bears all things, believes all things,
hopes all things, endures all things.
1 Corinthians 13:7 esv

Love is not fair, for that is not the point of love. Christlike love puts the welfare of others first. The Lord loves us and sacrifices himself without limit. When we act rebelliously or unfaithfully, he remains faithful to us and is always willing to receive us back to himself.

God's love, and the love he calls us to, is limitless. It is willing to bear anything. Love believes in others, even when they might not believe in themselves. It isn't gullible, but it chooses to reinforce the good. Love confidently hopes for the best, knowing that God will have his way in the end. Love is willing to endure anything for the sake of others.

Teach me how to love the way you love, Lord Jesus. With your eyes wide open, you chose love through the most difficult of situations.

Does Christ's love demand that you endure an abusive situation? How is love also discerning?

GIVE THANKS

*Give thanks to the L*ORD*, for he is good;*
his love endures forever.

PSALM 118:1 NIV

Psalm 118 was written during unbelievable devastation. Conditions were not good. David was in the middle of terrible times, with enemies encamped on every side, when he called out to God. He said he felt pushed back and about to fall. But even in this seemingly impossible scenario, he put his trust in God's faithfulness to protect him.

To emphasize the faith the psalmist had in God, he began and ended the chapter with the same message: Give thanks to the Lord, for he is good; his love endures forever.

Even during the worst of days, you are still good, Father. Your love endures every onslaught and will continue to last forever. For this and for so much more, I give you thanks.

What are you thankful for today?

SHARE

"Anyone who has two shirts should share with the one who has none, and anyone who has food should do the same."

LUKE 3:11 NIV

When we begin to truly see ourselves as part of God's family—members of one body, striving for the same purposes—then we might stop acting like individual members working only for our own achievements. Together we suffer and together we rejoice.

If someone else is cold or hungry, we should view it as if we are in the same family. They are sisters and brothers because God is our Father. Since every blessing comes from him, God wants his children to learn how to share.

Lord, I look around for those who are in need and honestly evaluate how I can help meet those needs. I do not want to assume that someone else will come to their aid and fail to act. It is my honor and pleasure to be able to love others in your name, and to be your hands and feet on this earth.

Who can you reach out to and help this week?

CROWN OF BEAUTY

To all who mourn in Israel, he will give a crown of beauty for ashes,
a joyous blessing instead of mourning, festive praise instead of
despair. In their righteousness, they will be like great oaks that the
Lord has planted for his own glory.

ISAIAH 61:3 NLT

God is so capable of taking something horrible and creating something beautiful. When we are sad, he offers us comfort and joy. He turns our despair into reasons for celebration.

In the middle of heartache, we should still seek God and trust him with our problems. He has a knack for mending what is broken.

Dear God, establish me like a strong tree, so that when distress comes upon me, I will not crumble. Help me trust you to make sense of the madness and to reestablish me once again. Please take my broken heart and give me a crown of beauty in exchange.

What might be an accurate conclusion if the Lord does not immediately alleviate your suffering?

GOD'S WILL

Be thankful in all circumstances,
for this is God's will for you
who belong to Christ Jesus.
1 Thessalonians 5:18 NLT

God's grace is more than sufficient to carry us through any circumstance. His love is unending and his mercies surround us every day. Understanding how great of a God we serve gives us a reason to be thankful always. Even when we are having difficult days, we should be filled with gratitude for all God has done. Hard times will pass, but God's grace never will.

Our thankfulness is also closely linked to the testimony of what God has done and how we represent the love we have received. When others see us being thankful in every circumstance, they will know that our joy is not dependent on good times but on a good God.

Lord, thank you for your abundant grace, your unfailing love, and your promises. Nothing is able to steal my joy or cause me to be ungrateful, for I know what I have received.

If you truly belong to Christ, how does that change how you approach difficult circumstances?

WHEREVER YOU GO

"Have I not commanded you?
Be strong and courageous.
Do not be afraid; do not be discouraged,
*for the L*ORD *your God will be with you*
wherever you go."

JOSHUA 1:9 NIV

After Moses died, the Lord commanded Joshua to cross over the Jordan River and possess the land. He reassured Joshua that there was nothing to be afraid of because he would go with him. Was it not, after all, God who commanded him to do so? Joshua listened to the voice of God, and he used God's Word as a guide, not turning to either the right or the left.

When God calls us to something, he will also provide a way. Our part is to simply follow him in faith. The more our faith is tested and God proves his loyalty, the more confident we become. Rather than allow obstacles to discourage us, we can be encouraged knowing that God goes with us wherever we go.

Just knowing that you are with me fills me with such courage, Father. You are all-sufficient and all-powerful. Whatever you lead me to, you will also lead me through. Give me the faith to follow.

How do you know God is with you wherever you go?

GUARD YOUR MOUTH

Set a guard, O Lord, over my mouth;
keep watch over the door of my lips!
PSALM 141:3 ESV

In one breath, David called to the Lord and praised him. In the next, he prayed that he would not be drawn in by evil. Our mouths should not be used for both good and evil, and David knew that. He asked God himself to guard his mouth because he knew it was the doorway to the rest of his body.

Just like a steering wheel can control a car, our mouths lead the rest of our bodies around. Our words are powerful tools which can be used for God or for destruction. We should be diligent about keeping watch over what is coming out of our mouths. God will help us if we ask, for we will not always be ready for every impending scenario.

Dear Lord, I pray that you help me vigilantly watch what words I speak. You have given me the power to hurt or help others, and I want to serve you not oppose your work.

What are some practical ways you can guard the words you say?

WEAKNESS

Each time he said, "My grace is all you need. My power works best in weakness." So now I am glad to boast about my weaknesses, so that the power of Christ can work through me. That's why I take pleasure in my weaknesses, and in the insults, hardships, persecutions, and troubles that I suffer for Christ. For when I am weak, then I am strong.

2 CORINTHIANS 12:9-10 NLT

It seems counterintuitive to boast about our weaknesses, but if God has ever intervened on our behalf and provided a way when we could not find our own, we should rejoice in it!

Our rejoicing can be multiplied when we share our story with others as well. In doing so, we boast of God in our weaknesses. When hardships come upon us, we have a unique opportunity to see how God will use them for our good and his glory.

I do not view life the way others do, Father God. I do not live for my own glory or selfish pursuits. Therefore, if I get to see you show up during my adversities, I welcome them and even rejoice in them! Thank you for being my strength and using my weaknesses.

When has God proven his strength through your weakness?

NOVEMBER

Prepare your hearts and minds
for action! Stay alert and fix your
hope firmly on the marvelous grace
that is coming to you. For when
Jesus Christ is unveiled, a greater
measure of grace will be
released to you.

1 PETER 1:13 TPT

OBEDIENCE IS BETTER

What pleases the LORD more: burnt offerings and sacrifices or obedience to his voice? It is better to obey than to sacrifice. It is better to listen to God than to offer the fat of sheep.

1 SAMUEL 15:22 NCV

God has always cared about the condition of our hearts. When someone serves us out of their dutifulness, it does not feel the same as when someone serves us out of their love. Likewise, God desires a loving relationship. He has never been impressed by religious acts or heartless obedience, but by those who come before him with a contrite heart who are ready to obey his words.

We can sacrifice all we have for God, but without love it amounts to nothing. What he wants is a loving family who is willing to do anything for each other and for him.

Father, I do not always have money or possessions to offer you, but what I do have I give you. I offer you myself—my whole life. Use me according to your purposes because I love you.

Why does obedience reflect the condition of your heart better than sacrifice does?

ABOUND IN HOPE

May the God of hope fill you with all joy and peace in believing,
so that by the power of the Holy Spirit you may abound in hope.
ROMANS 15:13 RSV

There is nothing worth hoping for in this life, for everything will one day pass away. The only one worthy of all our hope, who can fill us with all joy and peace, is God. Since we know what he has in store, we can face this life now with joy for what is to come and peace knowing that everything will one day be made right.

God sent the Holy Spirit to guide us and rekindle our hope for the age to come. He fills us with power to face any battle because we already have the assurance that we win in the end.

Lord God, my hope is in you. In every obstacle I face, my joy and peace continue with me because I know that the obstacle will one day be removed. You, however, are forever, and I am so grateful for that truth.

What does abounding in hope mean to you?

OVERLOOK AN OFFENSE

Those with good sense are slow to anger,
and it is their glory to overlook an offense.
PROVERBS 19:11 NRSV

People love to be offended. It is so prevalent that tolerance has become one of the most idealized principles. This sort of tolerance, which sacrifices growth and healing to the endeavor of never giving offense, is far removed from a godly form of acceptance.

As Christians, our identity is rooted in Christ; therefore, we may overlook offense. We should not be quick to pick a fight, to react in anger, or to be easily offended. We have more common sense than that because God is our moral compass not our own fragile egos. By allowing God to control our tempers and our words, we become more like Christ and less like the confused population surrounding us.

God, please help me to overlook offenses that people may hurl at me either intentionally or unintentionally. Help me to be grounded and sensible, realizing that my identity comes from you and it cannot be torn apart by the words of others.

Why does overlooking offenses bring you glory or earn you respect?

FIX YOUR THOUGHTS

*Fix your thoughts on what is true, and honorable,
and right, and pure, and lovely, and admirable.
Think about things that are excellent and worthy of praise.*

PHILIPPIANS 4:8 NLT

To simply attempt to forbid evil thoughts from entering our brains will not work. Instead, we must fill our minds with virtuous thoughts. If you try to get air out of a cup by sucking it out, the cup will burst. Instead, fill it with water. By filling our minds with holy things, wicked thoughts are pushed out because there is no longer room for them.

God has promised to guard our hearts, but we must be willing to say yes to godly things and no to those things which contradict God's good nature. Over and over the Bible makes it clear that God does the work of salvation, and then gives us work to do as well. Our good works, good thoughts, and good decisions are in response to his saving grace.

Help me to focus on those things which are pleasing to you. Oh Lord, I am inundated in this world by malevolent messages that cloud my mind and my judgement. Please help me overcome evil with good.

How can you focus on what is true and honorable?

HARD PRESSED

When hard pressed, I cried to the LORD;
he brought me into a spacious place.
The LORD is with me; I will not be afraid.
What can mere mortals do to me?

PSALM 118:5-6 NIV

Although the world's powers can appear indomitable, all the nations of the earth cannot stand against God. When we feel as if our backs are against the wall, or the pressures of the world are laying heavy upon us, we can call on God and he will answer us. He will deliver us out of our narrow confinement, the prison of our minds, or our earthly bonds, and release us into a spacious place where we can run free.

Even if God does not remove us from the trials we are facing, we can rest assured knowing that he uses everything for his glory and we will triumph in the end. The Lord is with us, and he answers when we call out to him. Nobody can steal the freedom and the joy that God gladly gives.

Whenever I feel stuck, you provide me with a way out. When my load seems impossible to bear, you reach down and help me with it. When other people seek to do me harm, I know that your loving arm protects me.

What are you afraid of?

VALUABLE

"I tell you, do not worry about your life, what you will eat or drink;
or about your body, what you will wear. Is not life more than food,
and the body more than clothes? Look at the birds of the air; they
do not sow or reap or store away in barns, and yet your heavenly
Father feeds them. Are you not much more valuable than they?"
MATTHEW 6:25-26 NIV

As if an entire documented account of God's reliability
spanning over the entire course of human history wasn't
enough to ease our wandering hearts, he also filled our planet
with natural examples of his dependability and devotion to us.

When we question whether the Lord actually loves us, all
we need to do is consider the care he provides the birds. We
are of far more value to him than they are.

Father, you have provided for me every day of my life. Your
testimony of faithfulness stretches as far back as humans
have existed. When I am tempted to doubt your closeness
or your care, remind me of the birds and the flowers.
Remind me, God, of how much more value you have placed
on me.

What do you see in nature that proves God's faithfulness?

TEACHABLE

Listen, my son, to your father's instruction
and do not forsake your mother's teaching.
They are a garland to grace your head
and a chain to adorn your neck.

PROVERBS 1:8-9 NIV

Fathers and mothers are intended to be a picture to their children of how the Lord cares for us. We do not always like rules or discipline, but caring parents enforce good behavior because that is what is best for their child. Similarly, God teaches us to obey our authority and remember the lessons we have learned because they will be blessings to us as we navigate through life.

Not all of us had parents that cared for us, but the proverb's point still insists that we do not despise the lessons we learn, that we remain teachable, and that we listen to those who are trying to teach.

Lord, please keep my heart humble and willing to be corrected. Let me never forget the lessons I have learned. Help me to pass them down to others and give you all the praise.

What lessons have been difficult for you to learn?

UNSTAINED

Pure and undefiled religion in the sight of our God and Father
is this: to visit orphans and widows in their distress, and to keep
oneself unstained by the world.

JAMES 1:27 NASB

Simply calling ourselves Christians, attending church, and participating in religious activities does not make us followers of Jesus. Following Jesus and living as he lived is what defines true faith. When we begin to act the way God tells us to, we will look different from those around us.

We are part of this world, but we are of a different kingdom. Our pursuits are considered as having little importance to the world. Rather than pursue riches, we seek to help the distressed. Instead of taking care of ourselves, we take care of others.

Lead me to those who are in need of help, Father God. Keep my eyes open to the oppressed and destitute. Help me reorient my values and live by the laws of your kingdom rather than appeasing the world's insatiable wants.

How can you keep yourself unstained by the world?

HEARTS AT REST

This is how we know that we belong to the truth and how we set our hearts at rest in his presence: If our hearts condemn us, we know that God is greater than our hearts, and he knows everything.

1 JOHN 3:19 NIV

When we feel convicted, it is proof that the Holy Spirit is working in our lives. If our hearts were hard and we did not care, it would be evidence that we have been pushing the Spirit aside. Christ is not welcome in a heart that feels no remorse for sin or does not wish to change its destructive ways.

There is no point in hiding our sin in our hearts since God already knows its condition. The best thing for us to do is to confess the sin, invite the Spirit's involvement, and seek to change. Only then will we find rest.

God, I want to find rest in your presence. When I am in sin, the light of your glory convicts me. Rather than hide from your light, I ask that you shine on me and expose it. I want to confess it and receive your help to overcome.

How does the Holy Spirit use your conscience?

CELEBRATE

They celebrate your abundant goodness
and joyfully sing of your righteousness.
PSALM 145:7 NIV

God is not a hype or a fad. He is not a popular celebrity who will fade in time from our memories, unable to hold the interest of our children, and unheard of by our children's children. God's name has been proclaimed on the earth throughout every generation, and it always will be.

God's people, old and young, rejoice because of who God is and what he's done. This spans all ages across the globe. We can celebrate God on our own, in our hearts, declaring his righteousness and singing his praises.

Oh Lord, you are more than enough reason to celebrate, for you have shown me your abundant goodness. I am filled with joy because of your righteousness, and I cannot keep from sharing it.

What have you learned about God from people older than you?

DELIGHTED

Your love delights me, my treasure, my bride.
Your love is better than wine,
your perfume more fragrant than spices.
SONG OF SOLOMON 4:10 NLT

More than wine, more than spices, the bride is desirable to her husband because of his love for her. The Lord cares about our hearts much more than he does our actions. Our obedience and dedication are an outpouring of the love we have for him.

Gifts and sacrifices do not mean the same thing if they are given grudgingly or out of obligation. Recognizing all that God has given us, and in response to his unending love for us, we should give back to him out of sheer joy with thankfulness and love in our hearts.

Delight in me, dear God, for I strive to be your pleasing bride. I will show my love for you in the way I speak and act.

When you do not want to obey, how can your obedience to the Lord delight him?

WALK WISELY

Be very careful, then, how you live—not as unwise but as wise, making the most of every opportunity, because the days are evil.

EPHESIANS 5:15-16 NIV

Paul had been beaten, shipwrecked, stoned, imprisoned, and homeless. He was well aware that any day could be his last. Although we may not have been beckoned by death as often as he, we also do not know when our lives will end.

Our time on earth is not just short, it is filled with evil days as well. Everywhere we look, unwise people live for themselves and reject the grace of God. Our lives should be led by the wisdom that comes from God so we can be pleasing to him and an example to others. When we live like this, we can make the most of every opportunity to witness to others.

Every day you give me is a gift, Father God. Please fill me with wisdom and help me treat each day as an opportunity. Help me not to be dismayed by the evil around me but share your grace with those who are without.

How do you walk in wisdom?

WITHOUT WALLS

*A man without self-control is like a city broken into
and left without walls.*

PROVERBS 25:28 ESV

It is not hard to tear down someone who can easily be pushed to anger. Someone whose temper has got the better of them is like a city that has been left unguarded; you can steal their joy and ruin their day with the most minor of attacks. They have not rooted themselves in the promises of God and are not taking hold of the strength the Holy Spirit offers to them.

In direct contrast, someone who has self-control and who is not easily angered is like a protected city. They have mastered their emotions and find their identity in Christ. They cannot lose their joy by feeble attempts from their enemies. They are strong and well founded.

Please help me grow in maturity and teach me self-control, dear Lord. When others try to cut me down, bring to my mind your words. Give me patience and kindness. May I repay evil with good.

How can you choose to believe God's promises and maintain control over your words and actions?

PROVIDING AN ANSWER

In your hearts revere Christ as Lord. Always be prepared to give an answer to everyone who asks you to give the reason for the hope that you have. But do this with gentleness and respect.

1 PETER 3:15 NIV

Peter told his readers not to be afraid to suffer for doing what was right. He said that if we insist on obeying God, our suffering would bring blessing. Instead of fearing threats, he said we ought to revere Christ in our hearts. In other words, we should honor him and serve him above all. If he really is Lord of our lives, then his eternal glory will matter more to us than our temporary suffering.

When we have this mindset, it will change the way we face challenges and act in difficult times. The hope that we have in Christ will be evident. Someone may ask where our strength and our joy come from. We can respectfully reply that our hope is found in Christ alone.

You fill me with hope, dear Lord, and you set me apart from the dizziness of the world. When others ask how I maintain my joy and focus, please give me the right words to say and a gentle and respectful delivery.

How would you answer a question about your faith right now?

HIDDEN IN MY HEART

Your word I have hidden in my heart,
that I might not sin against you.
PSALM 119:11 NKJV

Knowing the Word of God is vital to living a godly life. The Bible is God's will and plan, recorded so we would understand how God expects us to live. In living God's way, we experience an unmatched joy and fulfillment for we are doing what we were intended to do.

When we truly know God and we are familiar with what he has told us, our chances of becoming confused by false teaching greatly diminishes. It is important to not only read the Scriptures but take them to heart so we remember them for when tough decisions arise.

Sometimes I act out of ignorance, Father, and I thank you for your gentle compassion. Please teach me as I study your Word and hide your lessons in my heart. I want to grow in understanding and maturity so that I will not sin against you.

What issues have caused you to question your theology?
How did you reach a resolution?

NOT ABANDONED

"No, I will not abandon you as orphans—I will come to you."
JOHN 14:18 NLT

When Jesus was preparing to go back to the Father, he comforted his disciples with the promise that he would return for them. He was leaving to prepare a home for them, but his departure was only temporary. He died so that they—and we—could live with him as his beloved family.

We are not orphans for we have a family both in heaven and here on the earth. Jesus sent the Holy Spirit to be with us, to comfort and guide us. He also established a body of believers across the globe who worship him together. The Lord will never abandon us, not for a second and not for eternity.

During the times when I feel the loneliest, I will remember your words of comfort and promise. I am never on my own, for your kingdom, Lord Jesus, will reign supreme, and you have allotted a place for me within it. You accept me into your family, and you care for me like a child. I praise you, Lord, for your goodness and your love.

When you feel alone or forgotten, what can you do to remind yourself of the truth?

COVENANT OF PEACE

"For the mountains may depart and the hills be removed,
but my steadfast love shall not depart from you,
and my covenant of peace shall not be removed,"
says the LORD, who has compassion on you.

ISAIAH 54:10 ESV

There is no force great enough to thwart God's plans or make him change his mind. What he has promised, he will do. When tragedy hits, it may hurt God's heart but it does not surprise or overwhelm him. His love and his promises are certain, and we can confidently rest in him regardless of the condition of the rest of the world.

Even if an entire mountain were to fall into the sea, or the whole earth crumbled around us, we have safety in the arms of Christ. We have peace knowing that he loves us.

Thank you for your compassion, dear Father. Thank you for the covenant of peace you made with me. Although the enemy may attempt to undermine your plans or scare me, I know that there is nothing stronger than your bond of love. I cling to you amid the storm, Jesus, for you are the surest thing I know.

What is God's covenant of peace?

LIKE NEWBORNS

Like newborn babies, crave pure spiritual milk,
so that by it you may grow up in your salvation.
1 PETER 2:2 NIV

Peter penned a beautiful play-on-words here. Milk in ancient Greek was logikon which shares a root with the word logos, or word. So, just as babies crave milk, we crave God's Word.

Babies depend solely on milk for their sustenance. They cannot go a day without it. It is their very life source. Likewise, we live by the Word of God, for without it we are lost. We grow and are sanctified by the undiluted and pure Scriptures.

Dear God, I tend to desire things that are not life giving; things that only contribute to my earthly wants and cravings. Please give me a taste of your truth so that my appetite changes. I want to experience life with you rather than waste my time on a life that is focused on self-gratification.

What does it mean to grow up in your salvation?

RUN WITH ENDURANCE

Since we are surrounded by such a huge crowd of witnesses to the life of faith, let us strip off every weight that slows us down, especially the sin that so easily trips us up. And let us run with endurance the race God has set before us.

HEBREWS 12:1 NLT

The believers who walked out their faith before us provide both encouragement and examples to follow. They serve as testimonies of what God can do through people who put their confidence in him.

God does not promise us lives free of pain and difficulty. What he does promise is that he will be with us and give us the strength we need to run this race.

Before you, oh God, I cast everything that is hindering me from pursuing you. Please strip my sin and selfishness away and give me endurance to run after you. Thank you for giving me numerous examples of the people you have used in the past. Thank you for choosing to use me still today.

Who do you think of as a having left a testimony of faith for you to follow?

THE LORD'S DELIGHT

His pleasure is not in the strength of the horse,
nor his delight in the legs of the warrior;
the LORD delights in those who fear him,
who put their hope in his unfailing love.

PSALM 147:10-11 NIV

The Lord is not lacking in strength; our show of power does not impress him. He wants us to learn how to trust in him and rely on his might rather than attempt to muscle our way through life in our own strength. Humility is far more pleasing to the Lord than ability. Our skills and strength are gifts from God, and our humble love is our grateful gift back to him.

Both the mighty horse and the tender butterfly were created by God, both are cared for by God, and both reflect a side of his character. Even if we feel confident and capable, we ought to fear God and follow his leadership. This will be pleasing to the Lord and will keep us out of a lot of potential trouble.

Delight in me, dear God, and accept my humble allegiance. You are both powerful and good, and I take pleasure in following you.

How has God displayed both his strength and his tenderness in your life?

WHOLE BODY

From him the whole body, joined and held together by every
supporting ligament, grows and builds itself up in love,
as each part does its work.

EPHESIANS 4:16 NIV

With Christ as our head, we are assembled together by love to serve him and each other. If someone in the body is suffering, others should rush in. If one member is rejoicing, the rest of the church has cause for celebration.

We should not envy others' successes, try to outdo each other, or despise others because their role is different than ours. Each of us has been called by God, and we depend on one another to complete this calling.

God, I want to be someone who builds others up instead of tearing them down. Help me guard my heart and mouth. Help me play my part and convict me of my words. Keep me from gossip and slander and help me to be attentive to ways I can serve those around me.

What is your part in the body of Christ?

BUILD UP

Let us do all we can to live in peace.
And let us work hard to build up one another.
ROMANS 14:19 NIRV

It does not naturally occur to us to work hard for someone else's success. Our selfish natures coupled with the world's agenda entice us to focus on our own achievements. Yet the laws of the kingdom of God are often paradoxical to human tendencies.

God calls us to work hard so that others are built up. We are to make every attempt to live at peace, and we are to dedicate our efforts to ensure others are built up. This is not self-centered living; it requires a Christ-centered focus. It requires humility and an eternal perspective.

Change my perspective, Father God, and help me to recognize my place in your family. I operate as part of a whole, not as an individual, to serve you and bring glory to your name.

Is there someone you can help build up?

GET ADVICE

Listen to counsel and accept discipline,
that you may be wise the rest of your days.
PROVERBS 19:20 NASB

None of us like being disciplined, but God does it for our sake. He disciplines those he loves because he has created us for something far better than we can achieve on our own. We discipline children so they can be mature and wise.

Wisdom comes from God, so we must seek him to attain it. He teaches us from his Word, from experience, and from other people he sends to help us. When we are humble and teachable, we can hear God's voice more clearly.

Lord, I seek you for counsel today. I desire your wisdom more than any riches on earth. Even when I have to face discipline, help me to learn my lesson, listen to your voice, and walk wisely.

How can you choose wisdom today?

NO CONFUSION

God is not a God of confusion but of peace.
1 CORINTHIANS 14:33 ESV

In addressing spiritual gifts, Paul clarifies that the one displaying the gift should not be doing so haphazardly or in an out of control fashion. The gifts are subject to the control of the user, not the other way around. The reason for this is that gifts represent the manner of the Giver.

God is the one who distributes spiritual gifts, and he is not a God of confusion. His mantra is peace, and he expects his gifts to be used in this way. Peaceful people represent God not demonstrations of confusion or chaos.

God, you bring peace to the chaos, answers to the confused, rest to the weary, direction to the lost, hope to the dismayed, and purpose to those who feel useless. You create order where there is only madness. Only you, dear God, can fix this broken world. Thank you for your clarity and harmony.

Have you been confused about something lately? How can God bring peace to the situation?

UNFOLDING OF WORDS

The unfolding of your words gives light;
it gives understanding to the simple.
PSALM 119:130 NASB

The more familiar we become with the Scriptures, the more our understanding matures. The Bible is intended to be understood by everyone, from the scholar to the simple. We just have to decide to dedicate ourselves to its study and ask the Lord for wisdom.

Through the Word of God, we learn how we originated, what God's ultimate plan for our futures is, who we are, and what we were created for. Without God's insight, we are left to confusion and darkness. Rather than pursuing ourselves and temporary happiness, we should pursue our God-given purpose.

Your Word brings me so much peace and clarity, for by it I can understand everything else. My life makes sense and holds divine purpose. Even how I was designed was with intention. Help me not become confused by the mixed messages of the world, but to always return to your Scriptures to illuminate my understanding.

What has God revealed to you lately through the Scriptures?

GOLDEN RULE

"Do to others as you would have them do to you."
LUKE 6:31 NIV

Often referred to as the Golden Rule, the virtue of treating others the way we wish to be treated is universally recognized and accepted as solid advice. What isn't as widely accepted, however, is the verses prior and post this one where Jesus instructs his followers to love their enemies or to love when it isn't fair. He tells them to lend to others and expect nothing back.

Treating others well does not necessarily mean that we will be treated that same way. We are commanded to act this way regardless because it is how people will witness Christ's love. The kingdom of God is not about what is fair, otherwise none could gain access. It is about putting our faith in Jesus Christ, treating others the way we wish to be treated, and expecting nothing in return because obedience to Christ is enough.

God, you saved me when I was undeserving. Now, I serve others regardless of whether they are deserving or not. Because of the kindness you showed me, I will be kind to others even if it is met with cruelty.

How do you apply the Golden Rule to your life?

LIKE A TREE

Blessed is the man who trusts in the Lord,
And whose hope is the Lord.
For he shall be like a tree planted by the waters,
Which spreads out its roots by the river,
And will not fear when heat comes;
But its leaf will be green,
And will not be anxious in the year of drought,
Nor will cease from yielding fruit.

JEREMIAH 17:7-8 NKJV

Putting our trust in the Lord is wiser than finding security in anything else. It may be tempting at times to feel secure in a relationship, in a house, or with a steady income. Sometimes we even try to find security by controlling our environment. All of this is temporal. It would be like building a house on sand which shifts.

By hoping in the Lord and trusting his words, we find true refuge. When everything else is shaken, we will not be because our roots go deep into Christ and he upholds us. The winds of change can never change God's love.

Hold me close, Father, and keep me safe when attacks come my way. The might of the storm does not scare me because you hold me in your hand.

What does it mean to yield fruit?

ACCEPT YOUR GIFT

Do not neglect the gift that is in you, which was given to you
by prophecy with the laying on of the hands of the eldership.
Meditate on these things; give yourself entirely to them,
that your progress may be evident to all.

1 TIMOTHY 4:14-15 NKJV

Paul wrote to Timothy, encouraging him to use his gift of teaching. Of what profit is it to simply possess gifts if we forgo using them? God has invested a unique set of traits in each of us to reflect himself and to play an intrinsic part in his plan.

God will teach us how to use our gifts and offer us opportunities to put them to use if we trust his leading and guiding. It is important that we refrain from becoming jealous of someone else's gift and praise God for the gifts he has given to us, learning to use them for his glory.

Lord, rarely do I innately know the best use for my gifts; I require discipling and training. Teach me, dear Father so I am equipped to make the most of every opportunity I am given.

How can you learn to use your gifts wisely?

SMILE ON YOU

"May the LORD bless you and protect you. May the LORD smile on you and be gracious to you. May the LORD show you his favor and give you his peace."
NUMBERS 6:24-26 NLT

The Lord instructed Aaron, the priest, to pray this blessing over the Israelites. Within it is God's encouragement, reassurance, and promise. The prayer is more than wishful humanistic thinking; it is a divine blessing that announces God's approval and delight in the recipient. We still use it today to pray over one another.

The prayer is a reminder of God's promise that he will never forsake his children, for he is a good Father who delights in us and loves us deeply. He shows his children favor and bestows peace upon us. We can have confidence in our Father's protection.

Oh Father, how you love your children! Your love is not restricted to a blessing, but this prayer is a powerful reminder to me of who you are. Help me never forget even for a second how you show me protection, grace, favor, and peace, for you delight in me.

What do you think when you hear that the Lord smiles on you?

NEVER-ENDING KINGDOM

You are the Lord that reigns over your never-ending kingdom
through all the ages of time and eternity!
You are faithful to fulfill every promise you've made.
You manifest yourself as Kindness in all you do!
PSALM 145:13 TPT

There is nothing we can manufacture here on earth that will stand for eternity. Every earthly kingdom will crumble in time, and only what God has established will remain.

Why should we follow the foolish, short-sighted whims of the world, and waste our hearts and lives building fated kingdoms? Our calling is to a kingdom that will never end, and our investments into that kingdom have eternal worth.

Father, sometimes I lose sight of what matters and sell myself short. I stress and worry about the demands of the daily grind and overlook the importance of relationships and worship. When I take a moment to encourage someone or spend a little extra time with you, please remind me of how much value you assign those eternal investments. Thank you for giving me a place in your never-ending kingdom!

In what ways are you investing in the kingdom of God?

DECEMBER

The LORD your God is gracious
and compassionate. He will
not turn his face from you
if you return to him.

2 CHRONICLES 30:9 NIV

GOD'S PURPOSES

I know that You can do all things,
and that no purpose of Yours can be thwarted.
JOB 42:2 NASB

Job knew the Lord. He was a faithful and blameless servant of God who was upright in the eyes of his friends, his community, and even God himself. When he questioned the Lord's intentions, God revealed more about his holy character through a divine dialogue. As righteous as Job was, he was nothing compared to the goodness of God, and he knew that.

Job's response to the revelation was humble and submissive. He had been reminded of who he served and that his pain was not without a purpose. His concluding declaration was that God could do anything, and nothing could oppose God's purpose. No matter how upsetting or intrusive God's plans may feel to us, only he can see the bigger picture. We can trust him.

In faith, I will choose to trust you, God, for you alone can do all things. Remind me of who you are in my weak moments. It is an honor and delight to serve you.

How did God use Job's suffering for good?

AT ALL TIMES

Be joyful because you have hope.
Be patient when trouble comes,
and pray at all times.
ROMANS 12:12 NCV

We cannot fabricate happy feelings, but we can become so acquainted with the hope we have in Christ that it fills us with joy even in our sorrow. When trouble comes, we know that it will not last, so we can persevere patiently. God has assured his victory in the end.

Praying at all times offers the understanding that God is nearby and wants an active role in our lives. By conversing with him, living according to his Word, and taking time to listen for his voice, we can have our joy, hope, and patience renewed daily.

Remind me of my hope and renew my joy, God. I pray for your involvement and invite you into every corner of my life. Let me cling to you through times of trouble, for you are both my strength and my triumph! My struggle here on earth cannot begin to compare with the hope I have in you.

When you feel like you're lacking patience, do you pause ask God to remind you of the hope you possess?

SHARPENING

Iron sharpens iron,
so one man sharpens another.
PROVERBS 27:17 NASB

In ancient times, crafting iron took a lot of time because there were no electric sharpening devices. It required dedication, persistence, and hard work. Friendships should aspire to offer the same level of commitment. By investing in our friendships and interacting in an honest way, we create the sort of relationships that allow us to speak into each other's lives and keep accountable.

A few surface-level conversations will not accomplish sharpening. Devotion to one another through thick and thin, honesty, and integrity are needed for us to help refine each other. We must be willing to speak truth, but also put in the tough work of walking with each other through the growing process.

Sometimes sharpening can hurt, Lord. As I work out my impurities, I ask that you help me and surround me with others I can rely on. I also want to be a reliable friend to others.

Have you invested your heart and energy into key relationships in your life?

BRIGHT LIGHTS

Do everything without complaining and arguing,
so that no one can criticize you.
Live clean, innocent lives as children of God,
shining like bright lights in a world
full of crooked and perverse people.

PHILIPPIANS 2:14-15 NLT

The immediate context of this verse is in reference to those working in the church, but its intention is clear that everything we do should be undertaken without complaint. Disagreements will happen, but we should approach them with self-control in the pursuit of peace. The church is imperfect, people and worldly systems are imperfect, but we serve a perfect God and that should be the motivation of our hearts.

Diligence to be above criticism is important so we can shine like Christ. If we arrogantly boast, argue, and complain, we look just like the world. How, then, are others supposed to believe our message or find the road that leads to Christ?

I am sorry for grumbling about my work, dear Lord. When life is unfair or cruel, I will remember that I serve a kind and loving master. It is my pleasure to serve you and I want that to be reflected in my service here on earth.

Why does complaining and arguing counteract your message of the Gospel?

PROTECTION

Let all who take refuge in you be glad;
let them ever sing for joy.
Spread your protection over them,
that those who love your name may rejoice in you.

PSALM 5:11 NIV

The remarkable grace God gives us provides impenetrable protection and insatiable joy! Since we love the Lord so much, his protection makes us glad and we rejoice in it. If we did not understand God, we would likely not appreciate his protection. We would fight against his laws and act out in disobedience. Then, we would also be vulnerable to all the enemy's attacks and all the elements of the world.

The Lord's protection does not guarantee that we will be spared from pain or sadness. It is a safety much more lasting, protecting our hearts from failing and keeping our feet on the path that leads to life. Those who do not understand will attempt to build their own barricade, but for those of us who realize what God's grace entails, we have every reason to rejoice.

Protect me, loving Father, and fill my heart with joy. I will rejoice in your goodness and praise your name forever.

How can you show appreciation to God for his protection over you?

NUMBERED

*"Are not two sparrows sold for a penny? Yet not one of them will
fall to the ground outside your Father's care. And even the very
hairs of your head are all numbered. So don't be afraid; you are
worth more than many sparrows."*

MATTHEW 10:29-31 NIV

With all the evil in the world, it may seem like the Lord is
inattentive, but he is aware of every detail. He allows evil to
continue for a time in order to fulfill his loving plan, but his
divine protection is with all those who call on his name.

Even the natural world exists within God's care. He created
the birds, and it is he who cares for them as well. We are of
much more value in the eyes of God than the wonders of his
creation. Every one of us is so intimately loved by God that he
knows how many hairs we have on our head. He catches all of
our tears and hears the whispering of our hearts.

**Thank you for caring for all my needs and reassuring me
amid all my fears. Help me trust you more, for you have
shown yourself to be trustworthy.**

*Can you trust a God who understands you better than you
understand yourself?*

LISTEN AND LEARN

Wise people can also listen and learn;
even they can find good advice in these words.
PROVERBS 1:5 NCV

The point of attaining wisdom is not simply to be wise but so we can help guide and instruct others. God's gifts are to bless the body of believers as a whole not to elevate one individual. The first portion of this chapter instructs us to pass on our wisdom to others, and this verse summarizes that because of this mandate, we must constantly grow in our wisdom and understanding.

We are never too wise to learn something new. Often, God uses the unassuming to teach others, such as children or even a donkey! It takes humility to listen and learn from modest sources. Pride will be our downfall if we don't aim to increase our learning and find good advice.

Father, please continue to speak to me and teach me your ways. I want to be wise so that I can pass my wisdom on to others. Tear away my pride and open my ears to hear your truth.

Are you willing to listen to the advice of others?

ELEMENTARY TEACHING

Leaving the elementary teaching about the Christ,
let us press on to maturity, not laying again a foundation of
repentance from dead works and of faith toward God,
of instruction about washings and laying on of hands,
and the resurrection of the dead and eternal judgment.

HEBREWS 6:1-2 NASB

At times, we become unmotivated or spiritually lazy. We mull over the basics of the Gospel message and stay where we feel intellectually safe. This is not true growth, and like any relationship, we are either growing closer to God or further away. Relationships do not stand still.

The Old Testament laws were never intended to be the standard by which we could secure our own salvation. Their purpose was to reveal our desperate need for a Savior and to point the way to Jesus. To uphold them out of reverence for God is admirable, but to rely on them for salvation is misleading.

Continue to reveal yourself to me, Lord God. I don't want to become weary of your incredible message but constantly immerse myself in its truths so I am always growing closer to you.

What new truths of the Gospel have you learned recently?

NO FEAR IN LOVE

*There is no fear in love; but perfect love casts out fear,
because fear involves torment.
But he who fears has not been made perfect in love.*

1 JOHN 4:18 NKJV

The ability to walk in love without fear is a testimony of the faith we have in God. Although we sin, our sins are forgiven, thus there is no fear of punishment. We are in love with Christ and are reassured by his incredible love for us.

If we are afraid of God's wrath, it means that we have not understood his forgiveness and have not accepted his love. A good father disciplines his children for their sake, but he is always loving and forgiving.

Oh Lord, I am so immersed in your love that fear can find no place in my heart! I do not cower from your displeasure but embrace you like a beloved child. Thank you for delighting in me and forgiving all my wrongdoings.

Do you fear the Lord so you revere his glory?

WRITTEN

Your eyes saw my unformed body;
all the days ordained for me were written in your book
before one of them came to be.

PSALM 139:16 NIV

Our futures, just like our pasts, are in the hands of God. We were not an afterthought or a disposable extra detail. In fact, we were created for a very specific part in God's family, and we are irreplaceable in the eyes of the Lord. He made each of us from the outpouring of his love, and by his design we came to be.

During the hard days we can remember that the Lord has a purpose for those as well. Every one of our days are known by God and destined for us even before our lives began. The point of the hard days is not to just move us to the good days. There are incredible lessons to be learned and insights to be gleaned from every day we are given.

Thank you for crafting me and ordaining all my days, God. Remind me not to take them for granted but to live each one for your glory.

What gives you joy and appreciation for the difficult days in life?

SERVANT OF ALL

He sat down and called the twelve. And he said to them,
"If anyone would be first, he must be last of all and servant of all."
MARK 9:35 ESV

Jesus calls us to a higher standard of behavior, but he also demonstrated it with his own life. Immediately following his directive that those who desire to be first must serve everyone else, he took a child onto his lap and said whoever loves children loves him. Later, Jesus, the king of the universe, got down on his knees and washed his friends' feet.

The Greek word for servant is diakonos, which means to act according to the desires of others. Jesus put our needs and desires before his own. If we claim to be his friends and his followers, we must be willing to also lay aside our desires for the sake of others. We must take up our mantle as a servant and allow God to honor us in his perfect timing.

Jesus, you spared no expense for those you love. Coming to earth, living a humble life, and dying in my place is the grandest act of servanthood and love that could ever be displayed. Thank you.

How can you serve others today?

CHOSEN ONES

Put on then, as God's chosen ones, holy and beloved,
compassionate hearts, kindness, humility, meekness, and patience.
COLOSSIANS 3:12 ESV

As followers of Christ, we are referred to as chosen ones: holy and beloved. It is evident that we have been set apart and accepted by the Lord. With our new identities should come a shift in character. Rather than identifying with the world, we learn to be more like Christ.

Paul previously classified two sets of five negative traits: sexual immorality, impurity, passion, evil desire, and covetousness as well as anger, wrath, malice, slander, and obscene talk. Here, he now counteracts these destructive characteristics with five godly alternatives. God's chosen people should resemble these instead.

During my interactions with others, help me to combat anger with compassion, malice with meekness, and impurity with patience. I thank you for choosing me and I recognize the calling you have placed on my life. Please work in my heart to remove the evil and fill it with more of yourself.

How does your life resemble each the five characteristics listed?

PATH OF THE RIGHTEOUS

Follow the steps of the good,
and stay on the paths of the righteous.
For only the godly will live in the land,
and those with integrity will remain in it.
PROVERBS 2:20-21 NLT

There are always reactions to our actions. Verse 19 warned that the seduction of sin will lead to death. However, these verses promise that staying on the righteous path would lead to the land God promised his people.

If we live for ourselves, what part have we in God's inheritance? But God has promised wonderful things to those who follow him and strive for holiness.

I want to dwell in your land, Father God. There is nowhere I'd rather be than in your home. Thank you for providing a way for me and for leading me on the paths of righteousness. Help me to choose good rather than evil, to choose you rather than a life centered around my own desires.

How did the land promised to the Israelites also serve as a narrative for eternity?

OUTCOME OF FAITH

Though you have not seen him, you love him. Though you do not now see him, you believe in him and rejoice with joy that is inexpressible and filled with glory, obtaining the outcome of your faith, the salvation of your souls.

1 PETER 1:8-9 ESV

Peter spent three years with Jesus and had personally seen him after his resurrection. He commended the believers who hadn't seen Jesus and still believed that Jesus was the Messiah: the only way to the Father. He declared that the outcome of this sort of faith is the salvation of our souls.

When Thomas saw the scars on Christ's hands and his doubt was relieved, Jesus told him those of us who haven't seen him and still believe will be blessed.

Jesus, I believe that you are the Messiah, the Savior of the world. Thank you for filling me with a joy so great I cannot even express it. I love you and look forward to the day when I will see you face to face.

What evidence has Christ given so that even without seeing him you are convinced that he is who he says he is?

HELD

The Lord directs the steps of the godly.
He delights in every detail of their lives.
Though they stumble, they will never fall,
for the Lord holds them by the hand.

PSALM 37:23-24 NLT

When we rely on God, he takes us by the hand and keeps us from falling. We all have times in life when we stumble, but by following God's directions and accepting his loving hand, we are guaranteed to never fall. Choosing his path rather than our own is the first step to ensuring a safe walk. He directs the godly, but the greedy are easily distracted and drawn off course.

Every detail of our lives matter to God and he is aware of all of them. He delights in us and in our lives, for we are his creation, crafted for his pleasure.

Direct me, Lord, by your love. Take my hands and lead me in your way. I acknowledge that your way is better than mine, and I choose the path of godliness rather than the ones that lead to temporary pleasures.

How does it make you feel knowing the Lord delights in every detail of your life?

CONDEMNATION

"Do not judge others, and you will not be judged.
Do not condemn others, or it will all come back against you.
Forgive others, and you will be forgiven."

LUKE 6:37 NLT

The Lord requires his children to extend grace toward others, since he covered us with his grace. He judged us innocent because Christ paid for our sins. Yet, if we judge others, then we choose to relinquish God's forgiving verdict of us. As soon as we condemn others by holding them to their sins, we condemn ourselves and all our sins will be held against us.

To overlook God's command on how we should love one another is to decline God's love for us. His love is unchanging, but he will withhold his grace from those who withhold it from others. His Word is clear. The choice is ours.

Please have grace on me, Father, and I will treat others with grace as well. I will forgive others because you have forgiven me. Thank you for not condemning me but providing a way by your blood. When I remember the price you paid, I dare not offend you by condemning anyone else.

Do you find it difficult not to judge others? How does this verse help you with that?

HIGHER WAYS

As the heavens are higher than the earth,
so are my ways higher than your ways,
and my thoughts than your thoughts.
ISAIAH 55:9 NKJV

Although we plan our paths, we are not as wise as God. Sometimes we try to take matters into our own hands, and then we are disturbed when God turns the tables. Our priorities are often earth-bound, but his are eternal.

The heavens are higher than the earth and we cannot begin to comprehend the matters of the universe. In the same way, God's thoughts are much more vast, loving, and effective than ours. It is still our responsibility to plan for the future and be wise, but we should not worry or stress when God leads us down another path.

Help me trust you more, Father God. When things do not go the way I wanted them to, please grow my faith and remind me that your ways are far superior to mine. Show me your ways, God, so I can walk in them.

How have you found God's ways to be higher than yours?

FRUIT OF THE SPIRIT

The fruit of the Spirit is love, joy, peace, forbearance, kindness,
goodness, faithfulness, gentleness and self-control.
Against such things there is no law.
GALATIANS 5:22-23 NIV

These attributes are not a checklist for Christians to attempt on their own; they are evidence of the Spirit's work in us. When we allow the Holy Spirit to lead us and we submit to his guidance, these characteristics will show up in our lives. We must choose to live for God and for others rather than ourselves, which will lead us into this fruit.

The word fruit used here is a singular term in Greek. The virtues are not nine individual fruits that we can pick and choose from, but all together they describe the Holy Spirit and how he also helps us to behave.

Please continue your work in me, Lord, and receive the praise from my life. I pray for your grace when I fail and for your help as I continue to grow in my faith.

Do you see these characteristics showing up in your attitude?

FAITH IS EVIDENCE

*Faith is the assurance of things hoped for,
the conviction of things not seen.*

HEBREWS 11:1 NASB

Those with faith are not expected to cower in fear but to have confidence in the power of God. Hebrews offers testimonies of those who underwent extreme circumstances yet persevered because of their faith. That same faith is accessible to us because the same God rules our hearts today.

We have complete assurance in God and in the unseen things he has promised us. Clinging to this conviction is putting our faith in God. Furthermore, God makes himself evident to the world through our faith.

Lord, I know that you are who you say you are. You have shown yourself to be faithful and true, and I am assured that you will fulfill all you have promised. My faith carries me through the most difficult of times because I am convinced of your goodness and worthiness. Thank you for the examples of faith you have given to me.

Why is faith based on conviction and evidence?

KNIT TOGETHER

You created my inmost being;
you knit me together in my mother's womb.
PSALM 139:13 NIV

The Lord does not make mistakes, and he made each of us. We were intentionally made for an eternal purpose. The actual term David used for inmost being referred to the kidneys. In the days when he penned these words, the kidney was esteemed by the Hebrews as being where our desires and yearnings were born. So, David is attributing our deepest and most primary desires to God as Creator.

We were carefully knit together by God, including our desires, character, and all other unique qualities. Instead of sacrificing our desires on the altar of adherence, we should ask God to reveal his plan for why he created us the way he did. He has a specific plan for each of us.

Before anyone else knew who I was, you knew me. You were carefully knitting me together, creating my mind, designing my desire, and writing my story. I praise you for my life and for your love. I desire you above anything else.

What are some of your God-given desires?

GLORY REVEALED

Rejoice inasmuch as you participate in the sufferings of Christ,
so that you may be overjoyed when his glory is revealed.

1 PETER 4:13 NIV

Our lives before Christ intervened were empty, but he came on our behalf and gave us a purpose in his kingdom. We are invited to participate in his holy work. This includes his suffering and his joy. Peter earlier guaranteed his readers that those who follow Christ will inevitably endure suffering and that it should not surprise us. Here, he tells us to actually rejoice in it!

When we suffer on behalf of Christ, the purpose of our lives is enriched because we are joining in the work of Christ. His glory will be revealed one day and our suffering will not be in vain.

I long for that day when your glory will be revealed, Lord Jesus. Until that day comes, I will stand with you through the joy and the sorrow. Give me the strength to be brave for you and remind me that you will never leave me.

When does the Bible say Jesus' glory will be revealed?

ACCEPTANCE

Accept one another, then,
just as Christ accepted you,
in order to bring praise to God.
ROMANS 15:7 NIV

Because God accepted us in our broken conditions, we are also to accept other people. This does not mean we have to tolerate sinful behavior or accept wrong beliefs, but we are to accept them into our community and our lives.

A simple affirming smile is not what Paul is talking about. God accepted us into his family and has an active relationship with us. In order to bring praise to God, we are to treat others with the same sort of love and reception.

Father, I like the safety of fellowshipping with others who think like me. I do not always enjoy others challenging what I believe or disagreeing with the way I do things. But then I remember the amazing grace you showed me, and it encourages me to open my heart and my home to others.

How can you accept people who do not agree with your convictions?

CALM

Fools give full vent to their rage,
but the wise bring calm in the end.
PROVERBS 29:11 NIV

Even if we are angry and our anger is justified, there is a time to speak and a way to act that is honoring to God. Allowing anger to control us opens the door to all sorts of sin and rarely accomplishes anything more than furthering feelings of anger.

When Jesus was confronted, there were times he spoke controlled truth, and there were times he remained silent. In his anger, he never sinned. We are to follow his example and learn how to conduct ourselves in the face of injustice. Learning this quality will make us wise and lead to a calm resolution. Real progress can take place and change can happen when we submit our anger to God and proceed in a calm and wise manner.

Dear God, direct my steps and teach me how to control my anger. Set a guard over my mouth and remain the focus of my heart forever. Remind me that you have the ultimate power and you alone are Judge over all.

How can you stand against injustice while still loving the perpetrator?

LOVE FORGIVES

Love is not rude, is not selfish, and does not get upset with others.
Love does not count up wrongs that have been done.
1 CORINTHIANS 13:5 NCV

Rudeness asserts itself in self-expression and self-indulgence at the cost of others' feelings. Although we live in a world that celebrates individuality, love chooses to consider others. Selfishness insists on having its own way and is unwilling to yield to others. A loving person puts the needs of others ahead of their own.

Getting upset with others happens often when we begin to view them as obstacles in the way of our goals. Human nature wants to get even for the wrongs done to us, but love follows the example of Christ who forgave all our trespasses and wiped the record clean.

Oh Lord, please fill me with your love! Human love is immature and self-seeking, but your love is selfless and forgiving. Teach me to walk this way as well.

Who are you loving today? Who else needs love?

LOVE YOUR LAW

Great peace have those who love your law;
nothing can make them stumble.
PSALM 119:165 NRSV

Those who live by God's laws and learn the value of them have unexplainable peace. Nothing can make them fall because their foundation is sure. To write God's Word off as a mere book of rules overlooks the entire purpose of the law. His law is our guide to life.

God's motivation is not to command perfect obedience for the sake of exerting power over his servants. He calls us friends, and his desire is to guide us to safety like a good shepherd protecting his sheep. When we ignore God's laws, we stumble. When we obey his laws, great peace floods our hearts because our footing is secure.

I love your law, for through it you teach and guide me, Lord. Thank you for coming to earth, for your humble beginnings, and your sacrificial death. I praise you this Christmas because you came to fulfil the law. I love it because I love you.

Why was Jesus' birth, death, and resurrection the perfect fulfilment of the law?

KNOW HIS VOICE

*"To him the gatekeeper opens. The sheep hear his voice,
and he calls his own sheep by name and leads them out.
When he has brought out all his own, he goes before them,
and the sheep follow him, for they know his voice."*

JOHN 10:3-4 ESV

Many flocks of sheep may be held in the same pen at times. The gatekeeper stands guard at the entrance and only allows in shepherds whose sheep were held within. The shepherd would then call out, and the sheep belonging to his flock would respond and follow him out. They knew his voice because he was the one who always protected them and led them to food.

The religious leaders of Jesus' time refused to recognize his legitimate miracles or the power of his messages. They did not know his voice because they were too focused on themselves. The broken, sick, and lost people responded and were saved.

Jesus, please call to me and lead me. Acquaint me with your voice as I learn from your Word and take your messages to heart. You are my comfort, protection, nourishment, and good shepherd.

How does Jesus speak to you throughout your day?

TURN TO THE LORD

Seek the LORD while you can find him.
Call on him now while he is near.
Let the wicked change their ways
and banish the very thought of doing wrong.
Let them turn to the LORD that he may have mercy on them.
Yes, turn to our God, for he will forgive generously.

ISAIAH 55:6-7 NLT

God loves even the wicked. We were wicked before he washed us clean and changed our hearts. There is no better time to call out to Jesus, confess sins, and rededicate ourselves to him than right now. He would rather we come to him broken and contrite than wait until we feel like we're in a better place. He wants to help us overcome our obstacles.

The Lord is abundantly merciful and generous. He does not hold our pasts against us, and he expects us to let them go as well. If we are willing to turn to him, he is able to turn us from our wicked ways.

My heart ponders wicked things, God, but you redeem even my thoughts. You know my darkest feelings and you love me still. I turn to you today and ask for your mercy and forgiveness. Thank you for showing me grace and turning me from my wicked ways.

What does turning to God entail for you?

TRADITIONS

*Stand firm and hold to the traditions that you were taught by us,
either by our spoken word or by our letter.*

2 THESSALONIANS 2:15 ESV

Many of the churches Paul wrote to had drifted from
their love for God. Either they had been persuaded by false
teachers or they had been swept up in their own selfish
desires. He now warned the Thessalonians to hold fast to what
they had been taught.

Some religious cultural traditions can impede the Gospel
and the spread of God's love, but many are rooted in Biblical
truth. These are the ones the enemy tries to distort and get us to
doubt. The way we can know the difference is by spending time
in the Word of God. We need discernment and we need to hold
fast to the Biblical traditions that have been passed on to us.

**Lord, as I study your Word, please give me discernment to
know what is of you. I pray that anything that isn't of you
falls away. I will listen to your voice before all the cultural
voices around me.**

*What are some Biblical traditions that the culture tries to
twist?*

GENERATIONS

*"Know therefore that the L*ORD *your God is God; he is the faithful God, keeping his covenant of love to a thousand generations of those who love him and keep his commandments."*

DEUTERONOMY 7:9 NIV

Our hearts are safe waiting on the Lord. He will remain faithful always because that is his character. He is loving, and he showers obedience with blessings. When we obey his commandments, he pours love on us, on our children because of us, and even across a thousand generations.

Although the Lord did not owe his people a single thing, he bound himself to a covenant with them. He will always uphold this covenant and remain loyal to us, even though we have broken our end of it and repeatedly been disloyal to him. When we do obey his laws out of love for him, he generously bestows blessings on us.

God, I praise you for upholding your covenant of love, even though I have failed you often. I will continue to pursue you and ask that you help me in my weaknesses. Reestablish me in your love when I fail you.

Why would God reward others for your obedience?

SHOUTS OF JOY

Then our mouth was filled with laughter,
and our tongue with shouts of joy;
then they said among the nations,
"The LORD has done great things for them."
PSALM 126:2 ESV

When the Lord restored the Israelites back to their home city, Zion, it was like a dream coming true for them! They had been in captivity for a long time as a result of their disobedience. However, the Lord is always willing to forgive and reestablish his children with his amazing grace.

Although the Israelites had gone out in tears, they came back laughing, shouting, and praising God. They understood both the grief of sin and the power of God's forgiveness. Their sin had resulted in slavery, but the Lord restored their freedom and led them back home.

By your hand, Lord, I am free. My sin weighs me down and enslaves me, but you step in and break its chains. You guide me back to the light, and I am filled with joy and laughter. You have truly done great things for me, and I will faithfully tell others of how you set me free.

When the Lord forgives your sin and picks you back up, do you praise him for it and share his goodness with others?

HOME

We are fully confident, and we would rather be away from these earthly bodies, for then we will be at home with the Lord. So whether we are here in this body or away from this body, our goal is to please him.

2 Corinthians 5:8-9 nlt

Paul knew that his home was with Jesus in eternity. He was not suicidal or seeking death; in fact, he was quite the opposite. He knew that his eternal home was secure, and this gave him courage and the desire to please the Lord in his earthly life.

Paul's point was that his true and lasting home was not this one, and that he was ready to be taken home to Christ whenever God decided it was time. Whether in heaven or on earth, his life's purpose was to be pleasing to God.

I want to be pleasing to you in everything I do and say. Father, I try to be a good follower and obedient child, but I often fail. When I do, please help me get back up. Thank you for loving me nonetheless and for preparing me a home with you one day.

Does understanding how much more glorious your resurrected body will be give you confidence in this life?